Wonderful

Summer

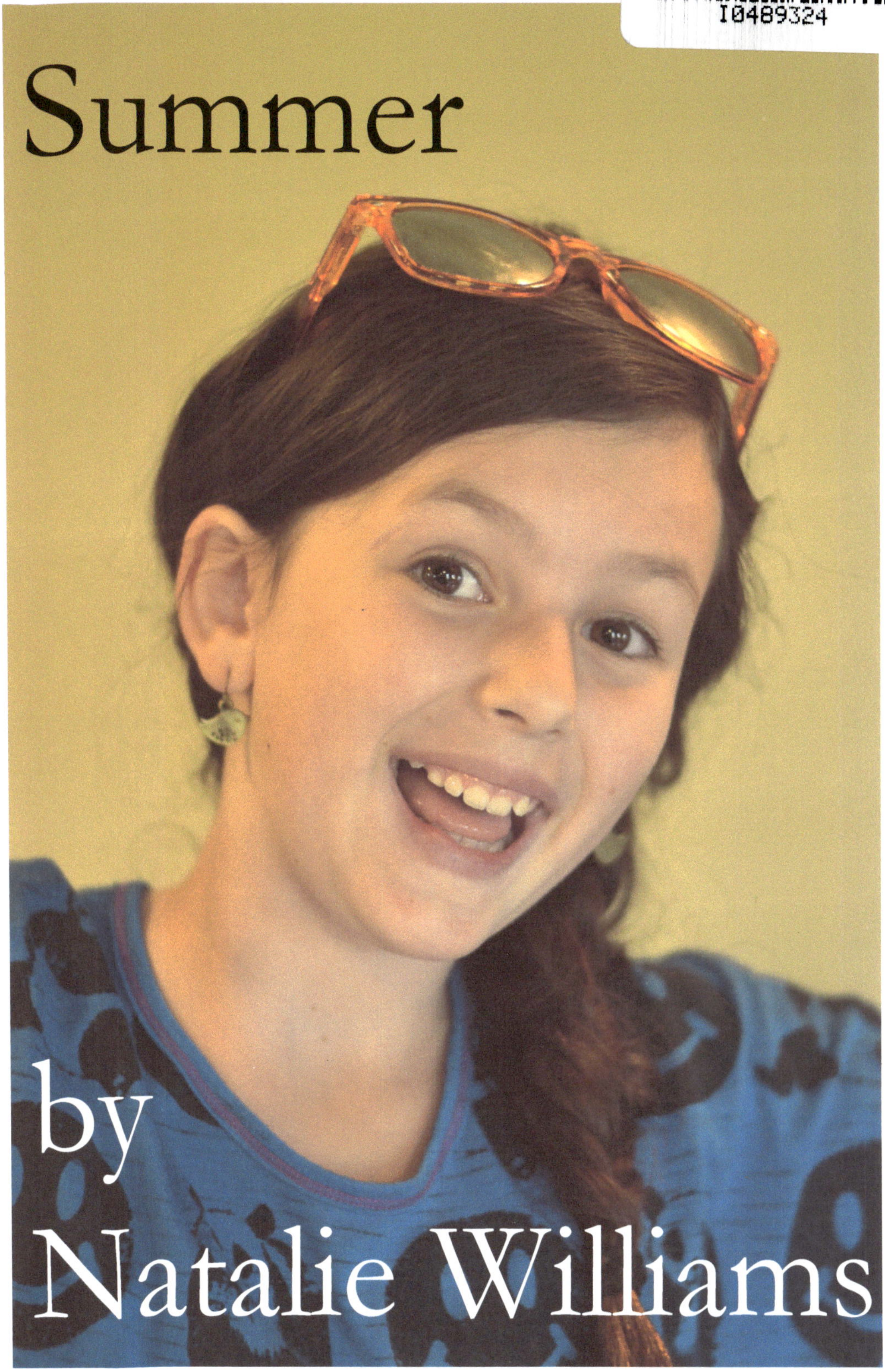

by

Natalie Williams

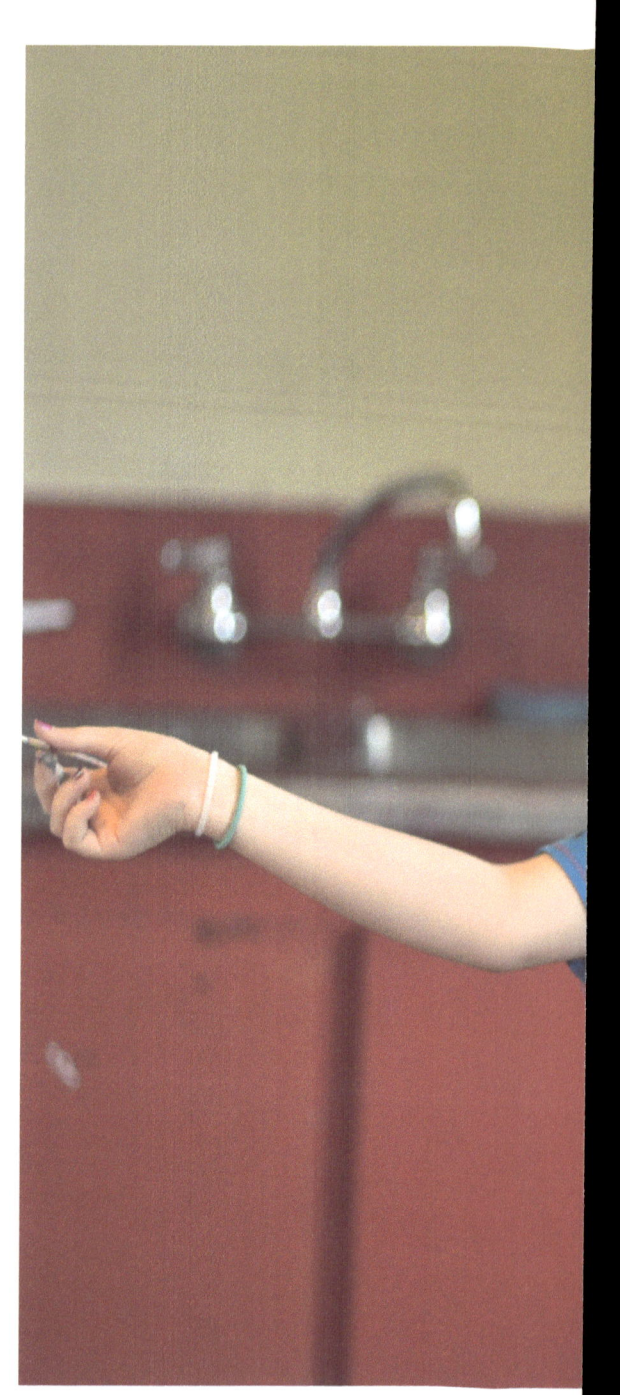

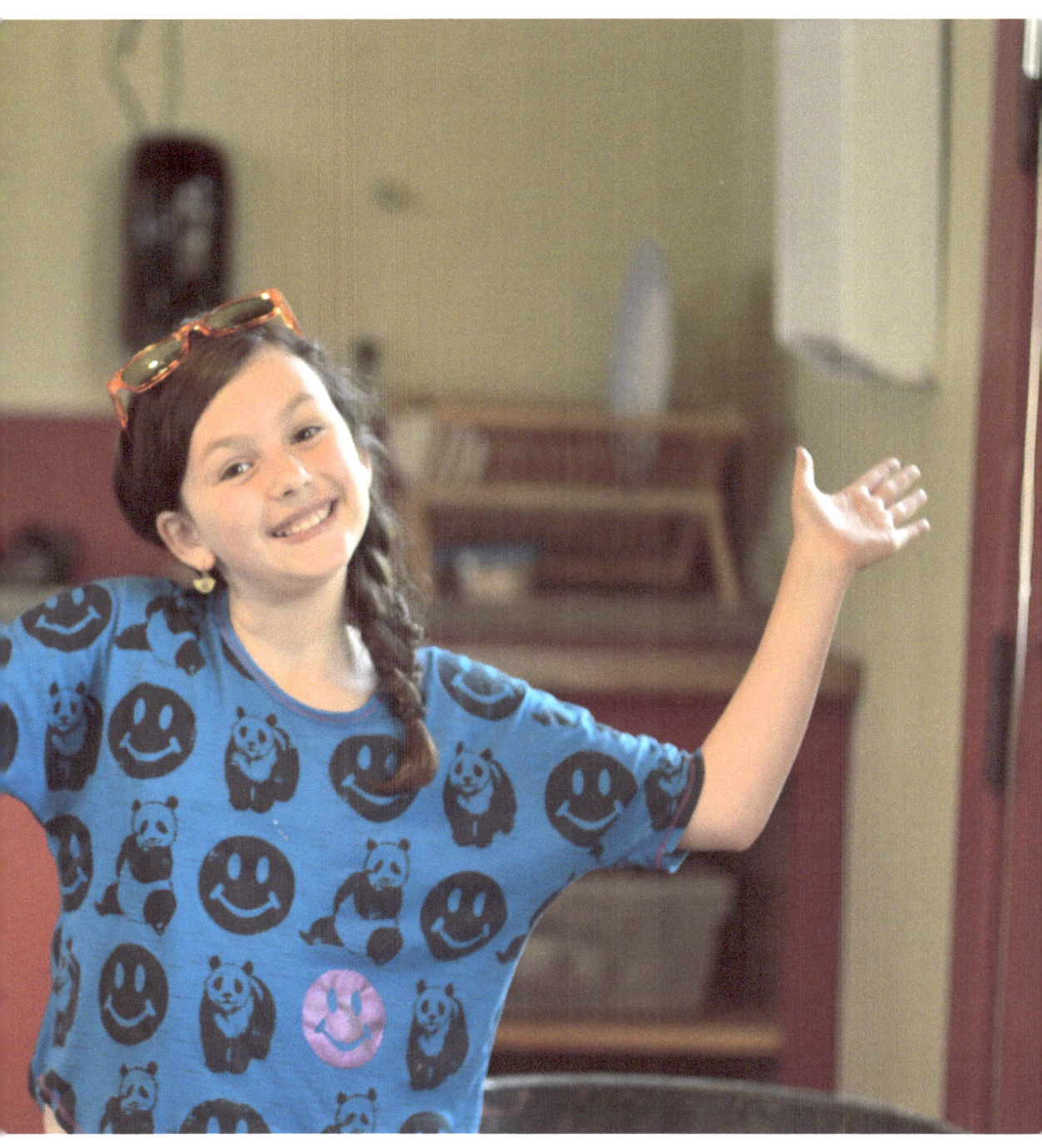

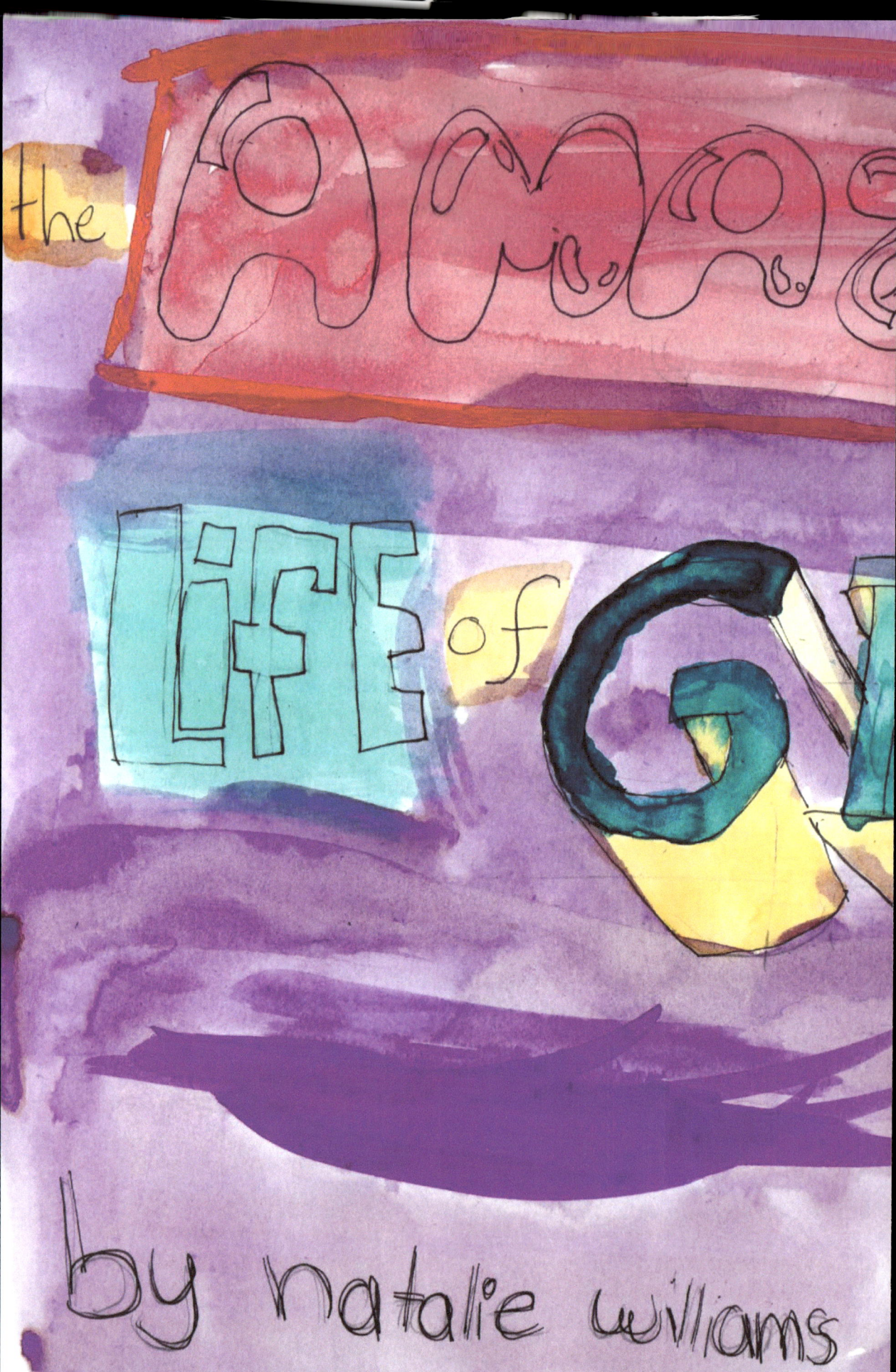

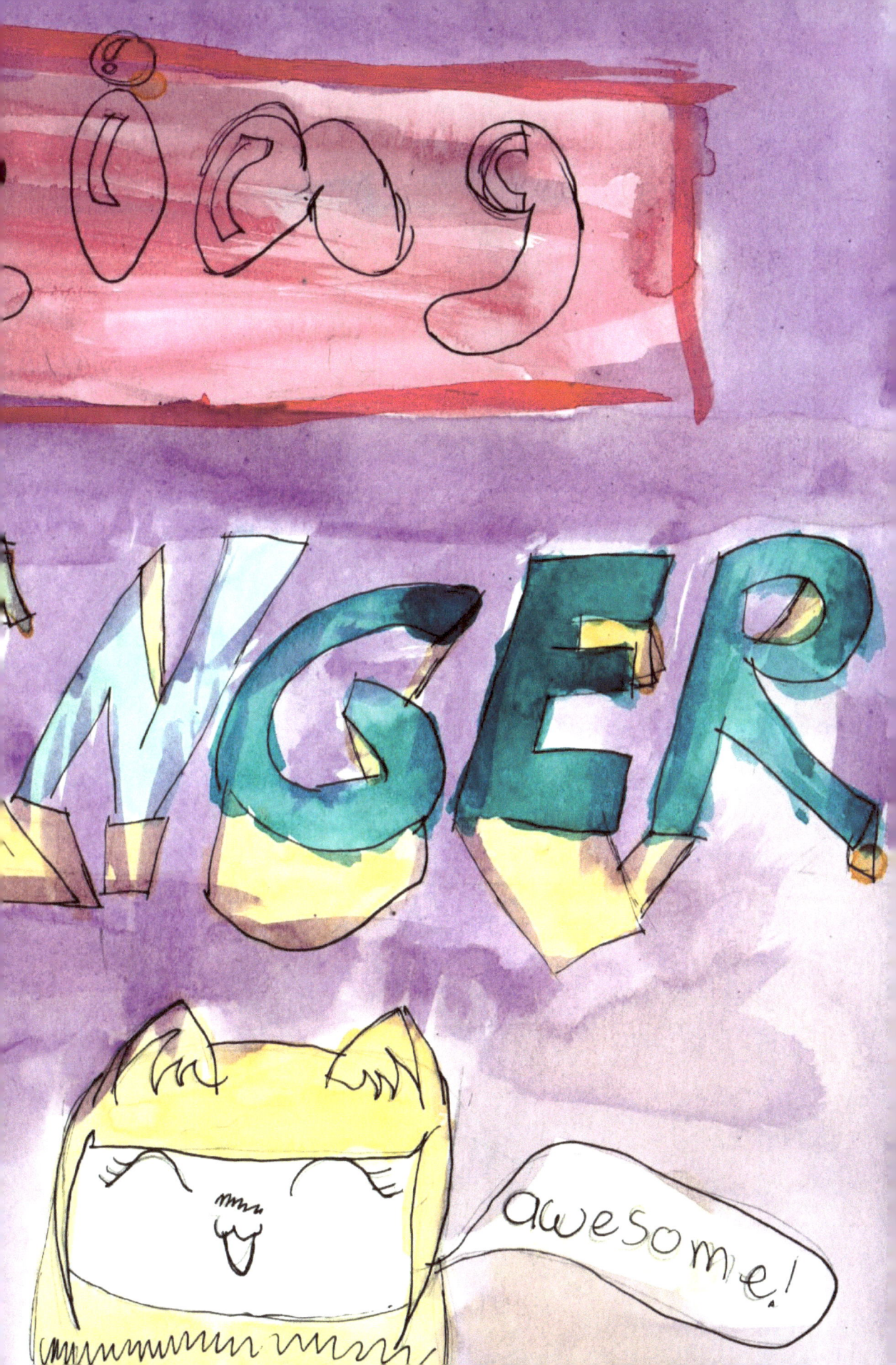

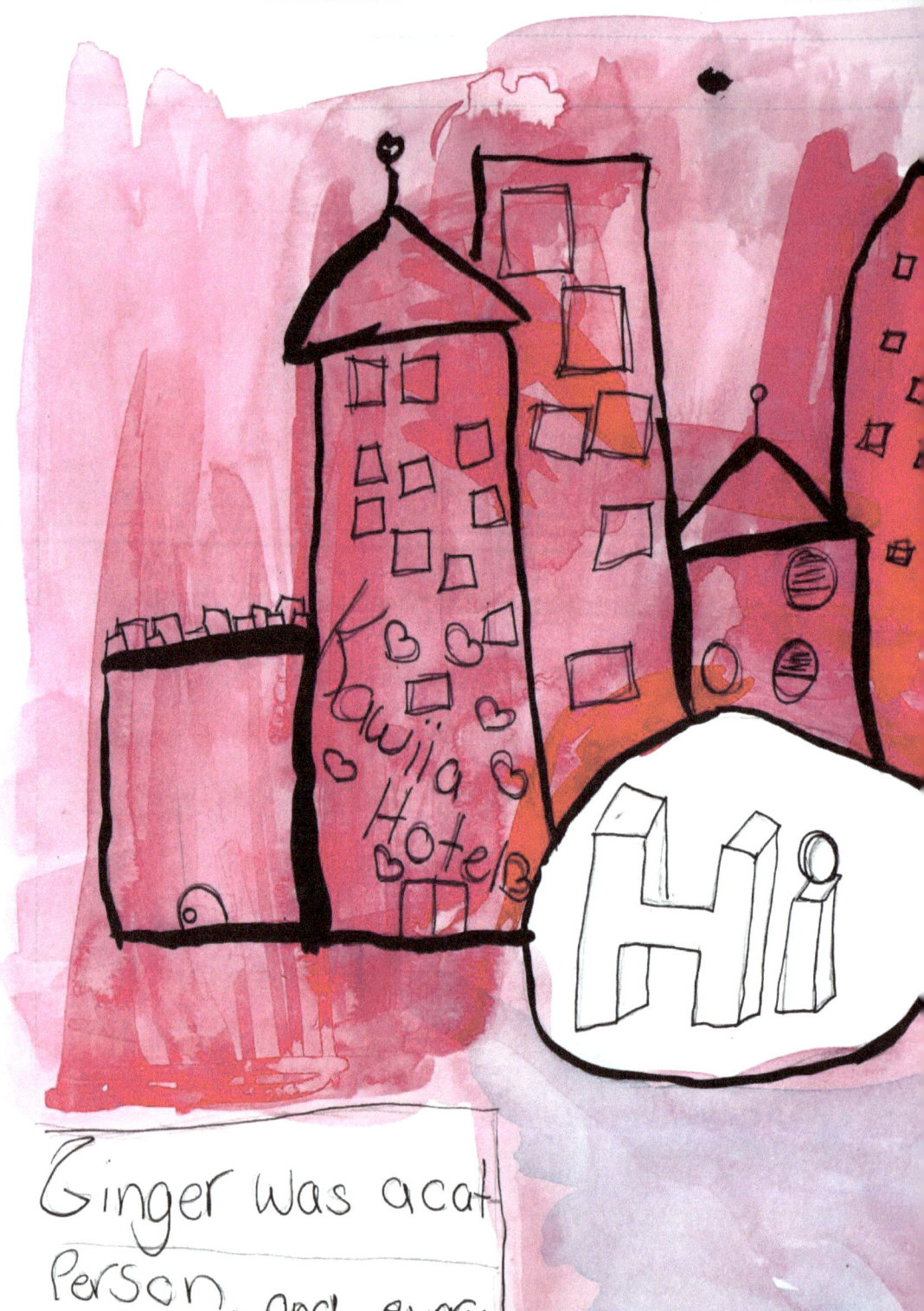

Ginger was a cat person, and every one liked and new her.

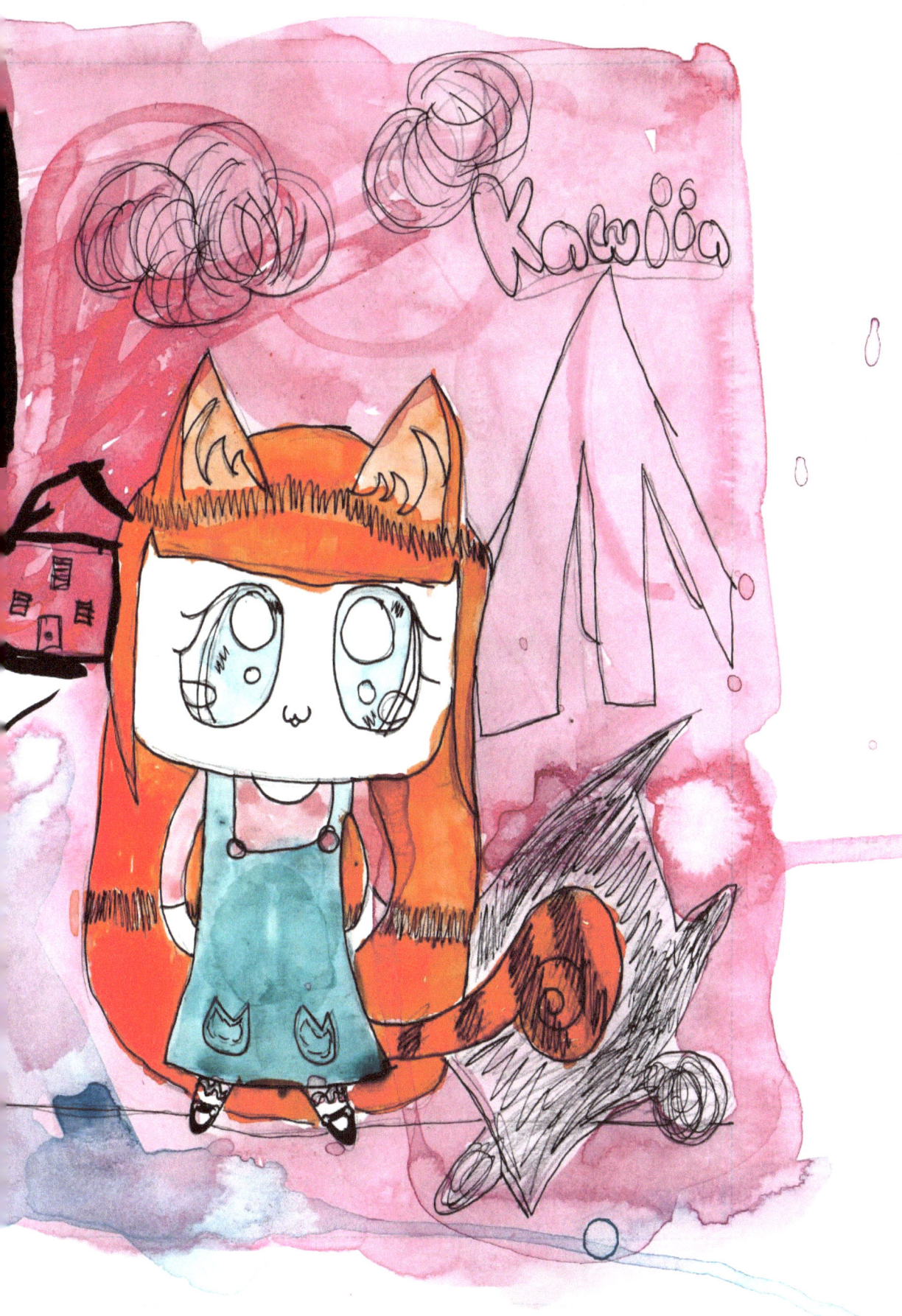

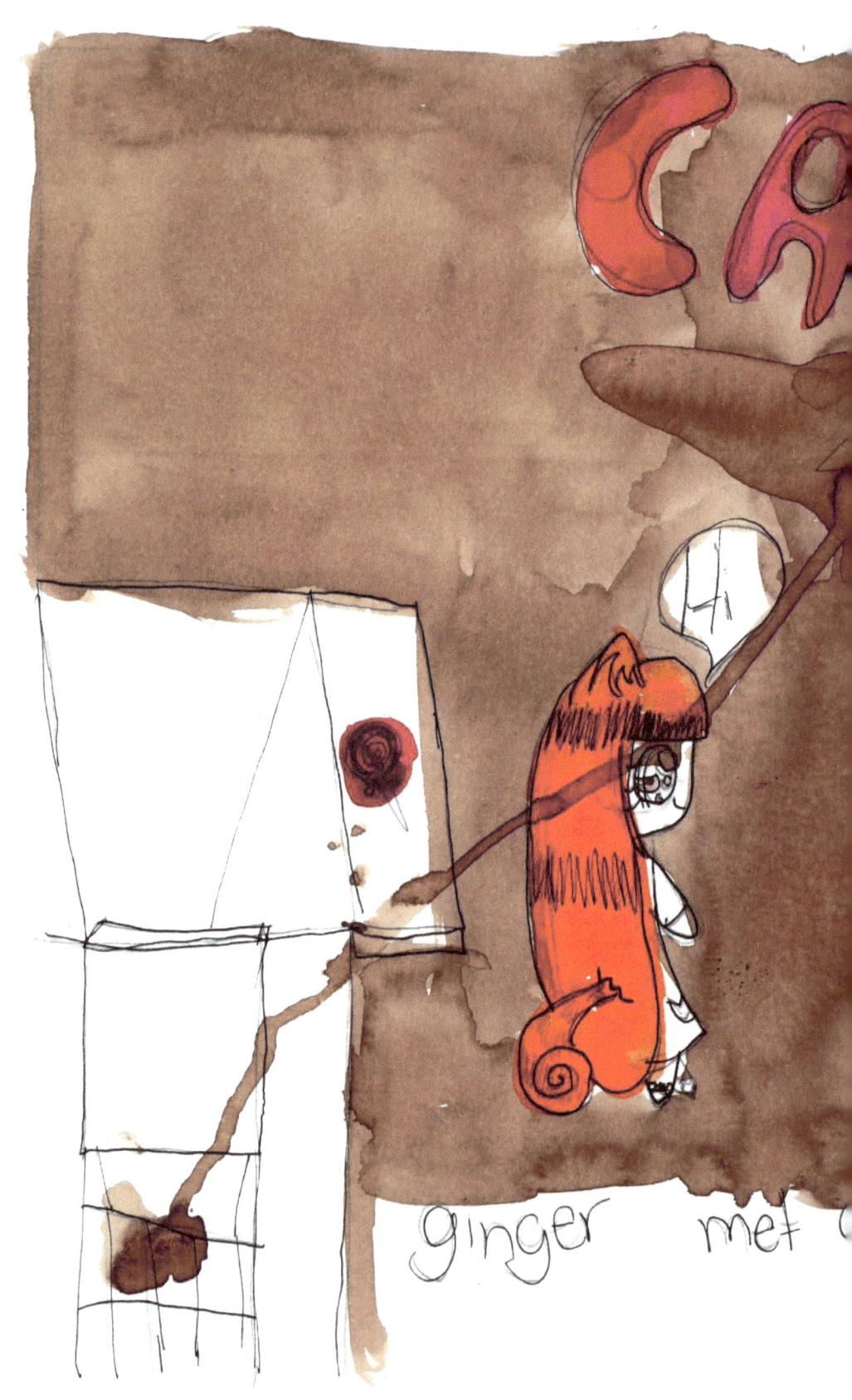

ginger met

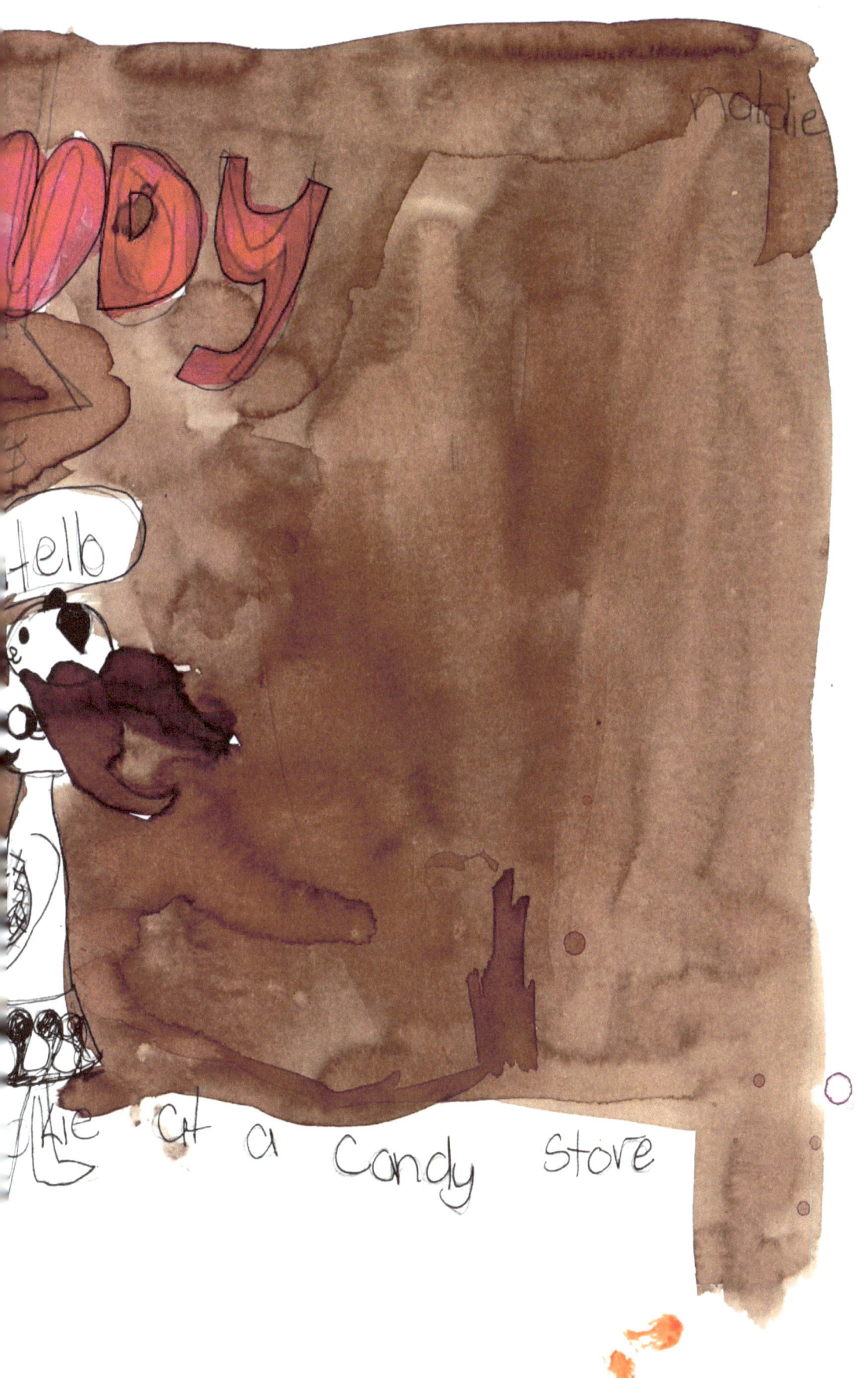

mr fish wanted her
her and took her un

...ame and run...

the sea

Help!

cookie le[d]

and night ar[]

she

met

ed reached all day
asked everyone

W ON

Scha

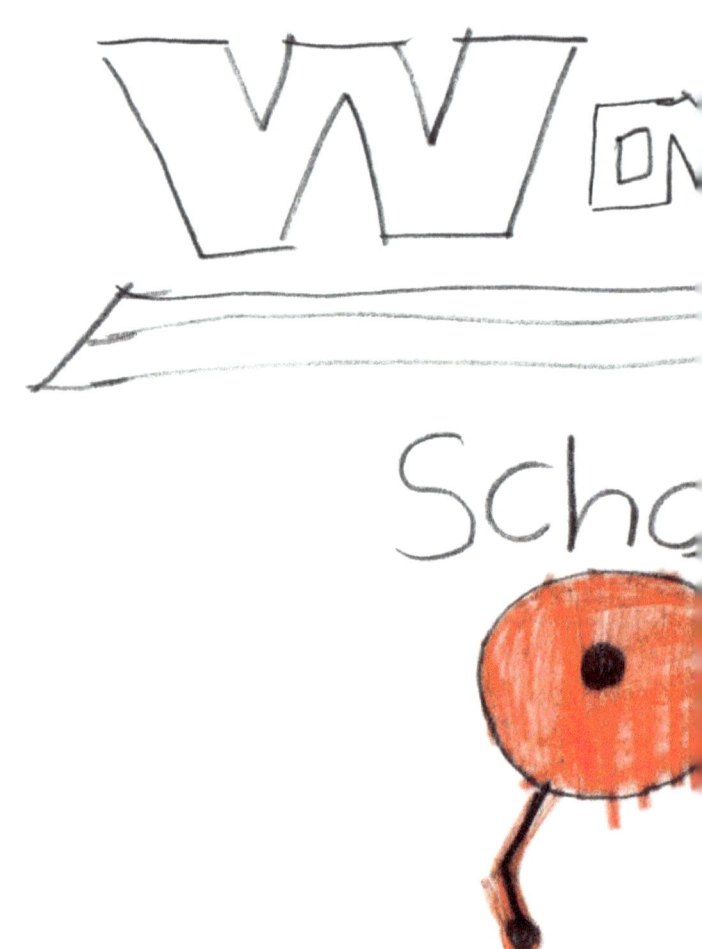

by: __zack KenneD__

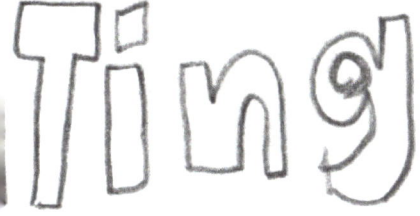

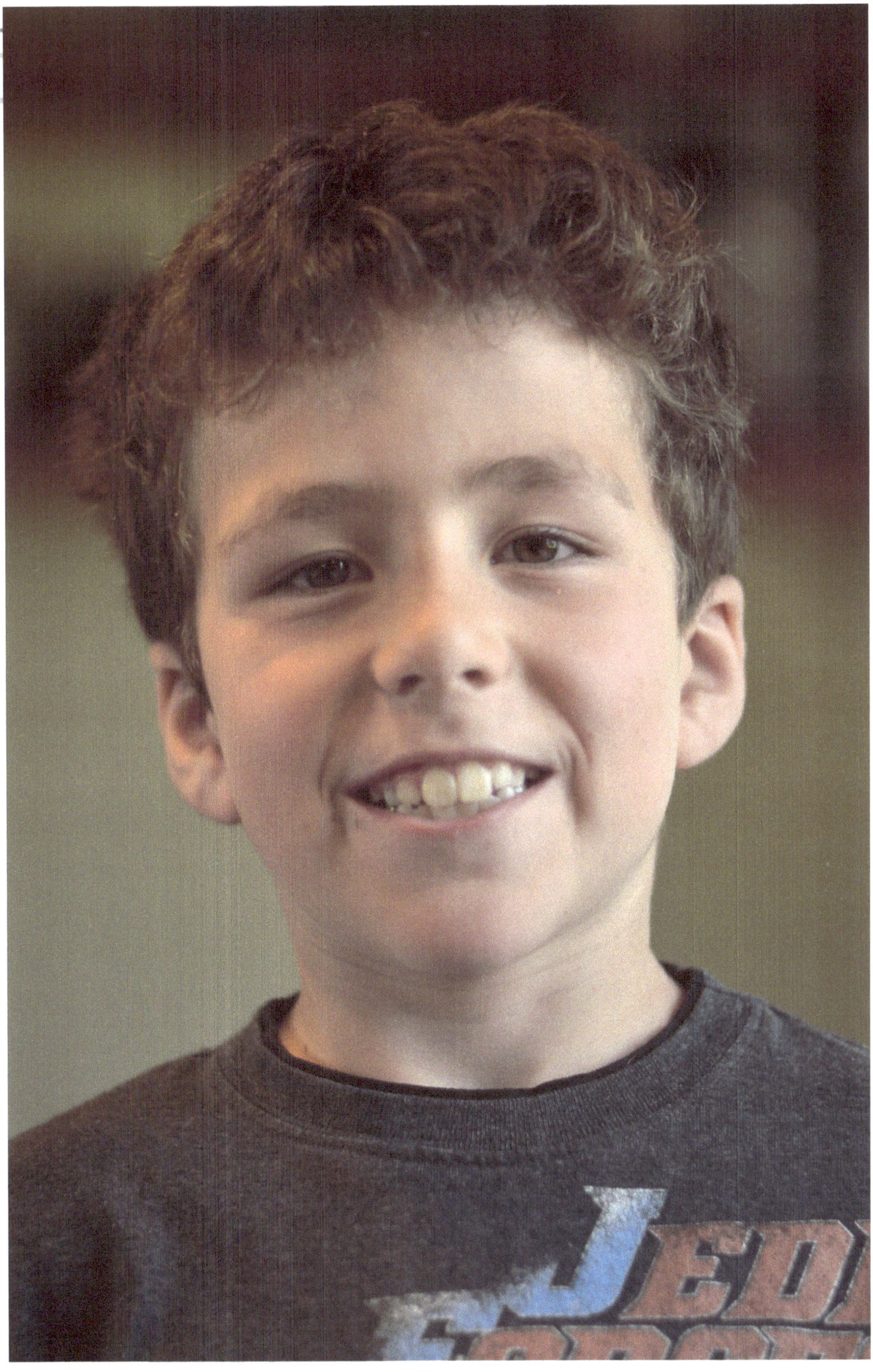

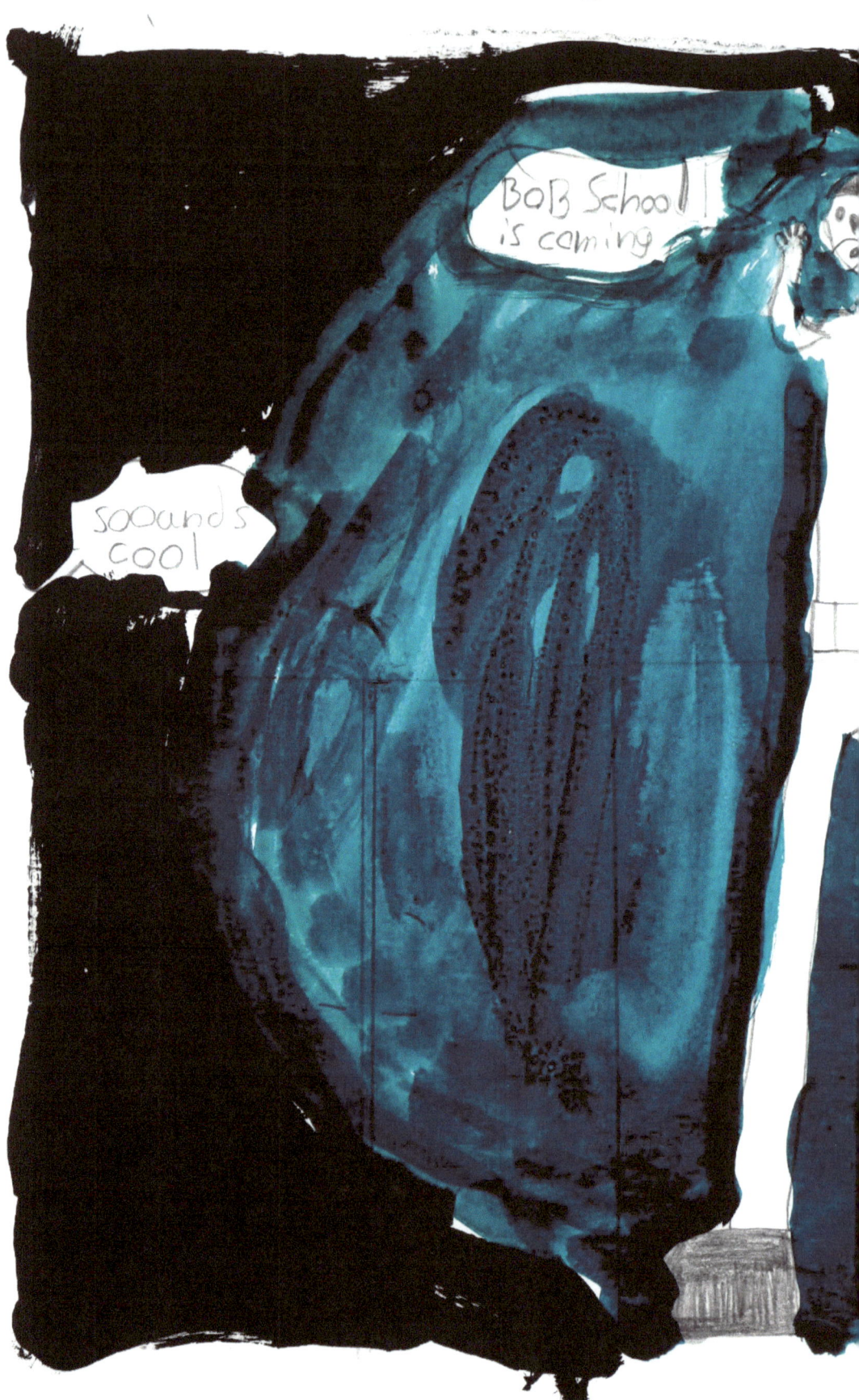

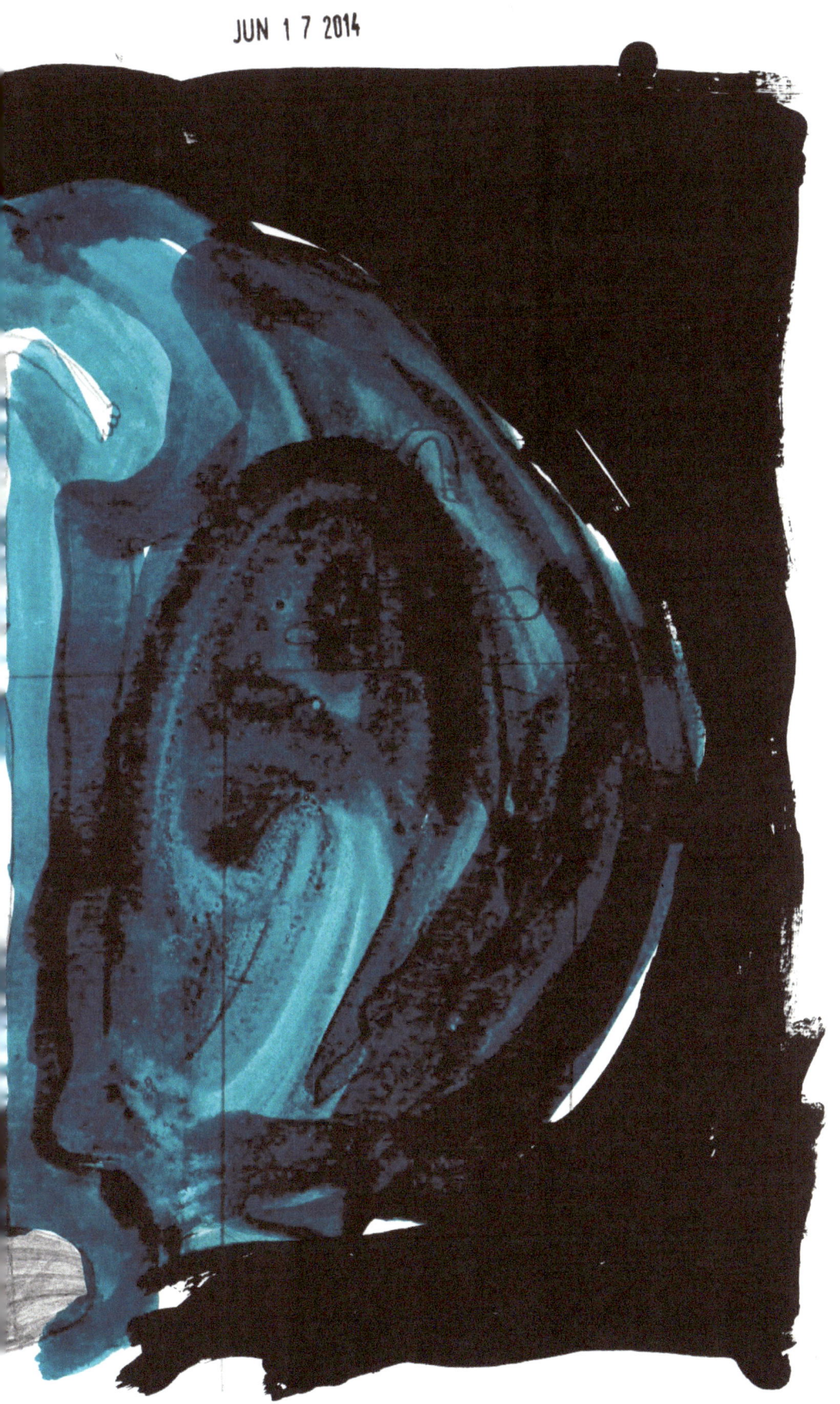

JUN 1

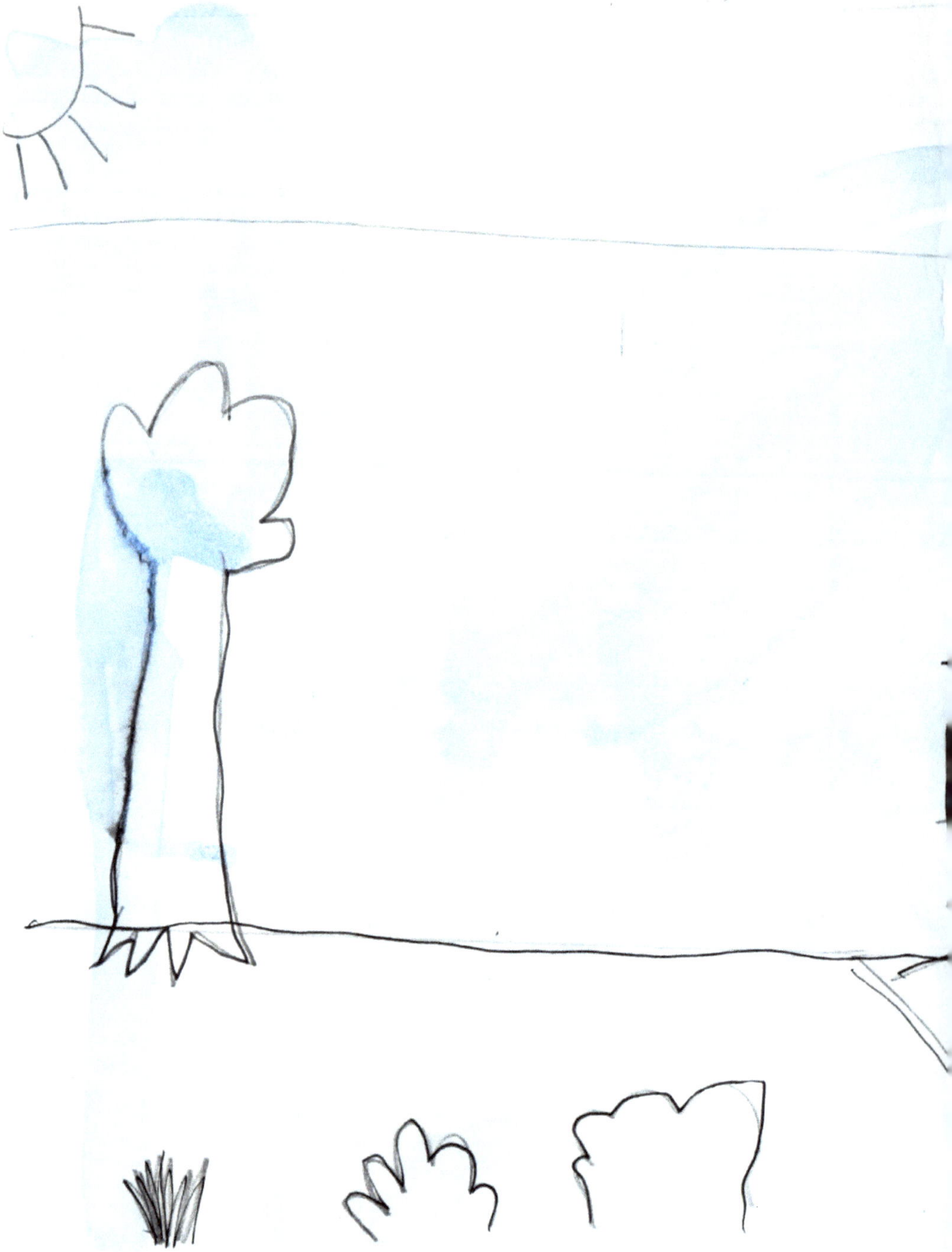

7 week's
later
septembe 3
8:30

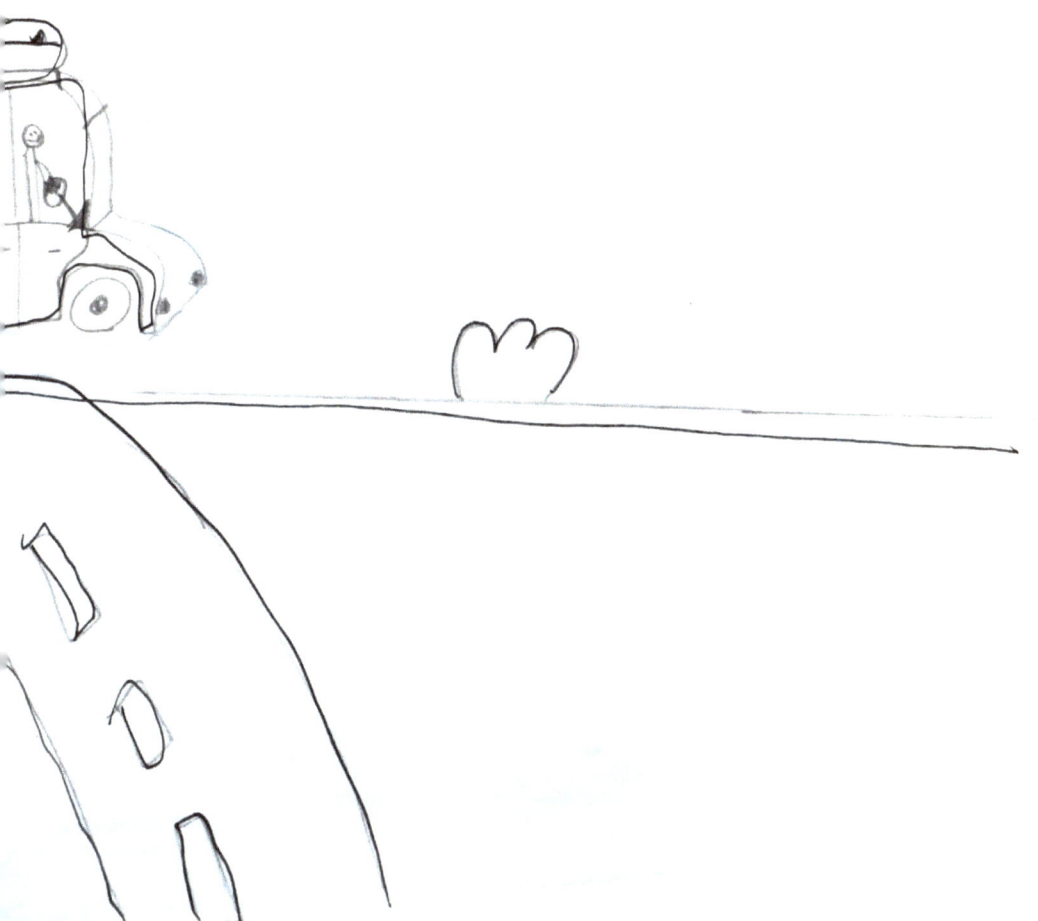

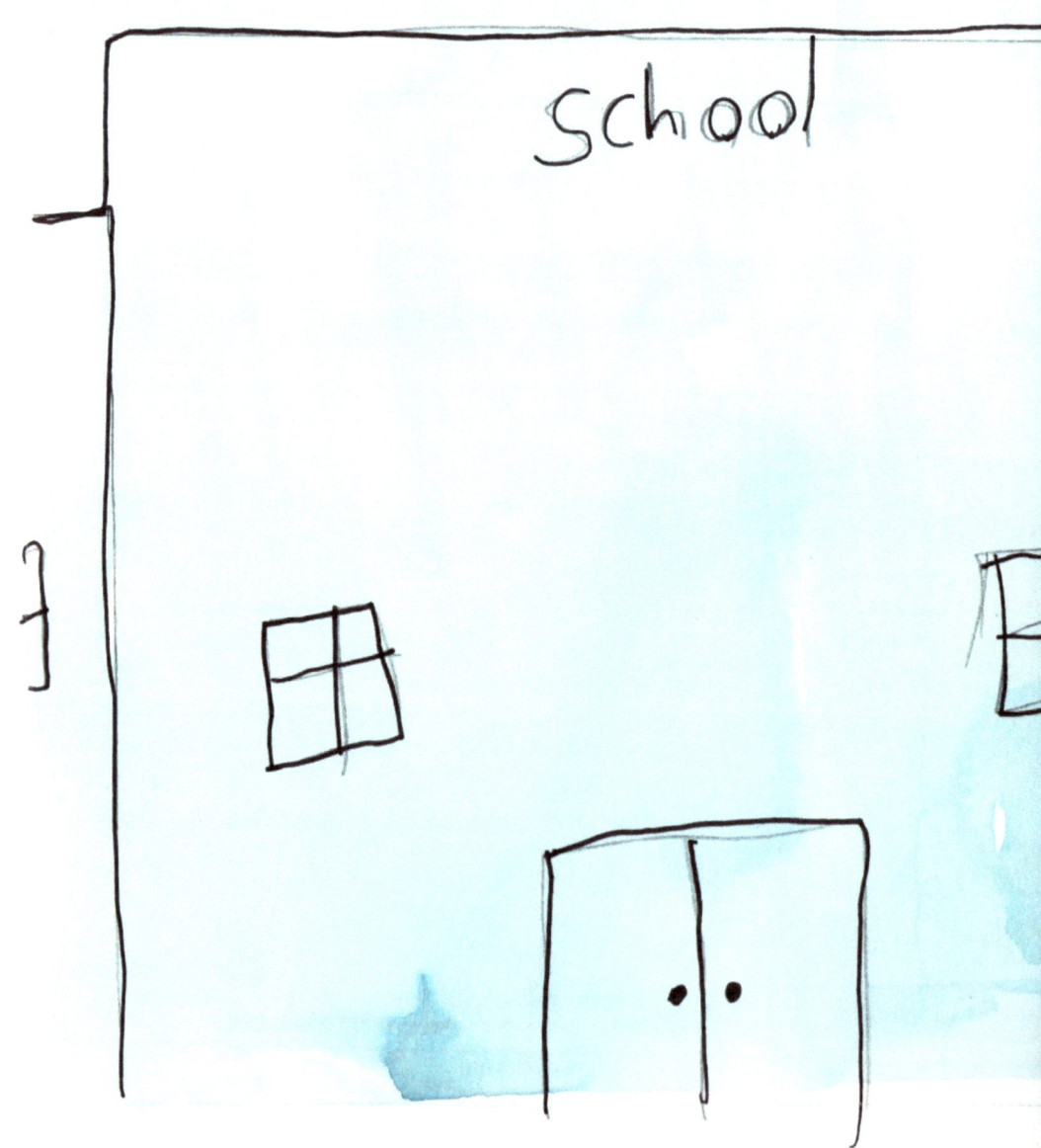

School

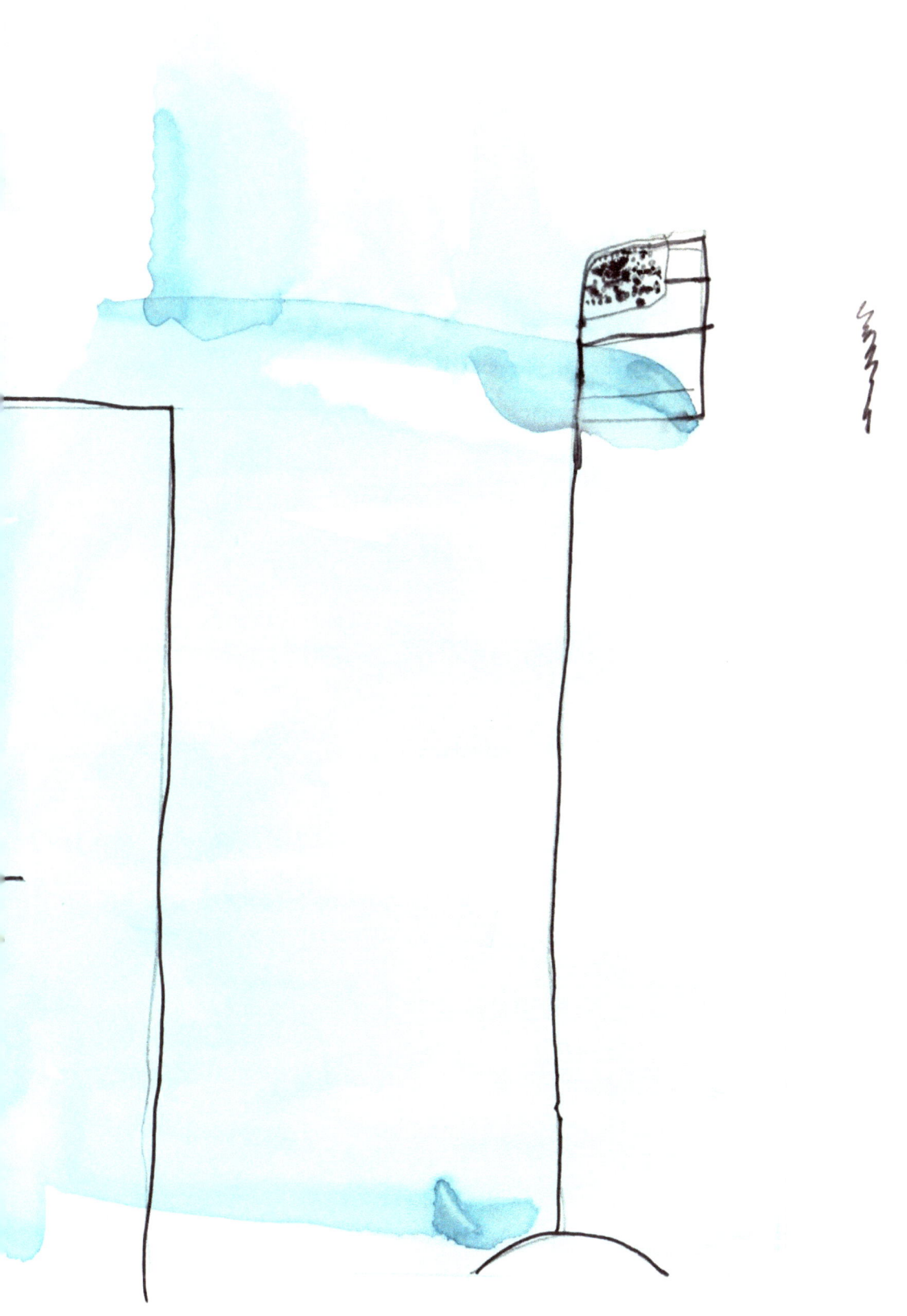

JUN 19 2014

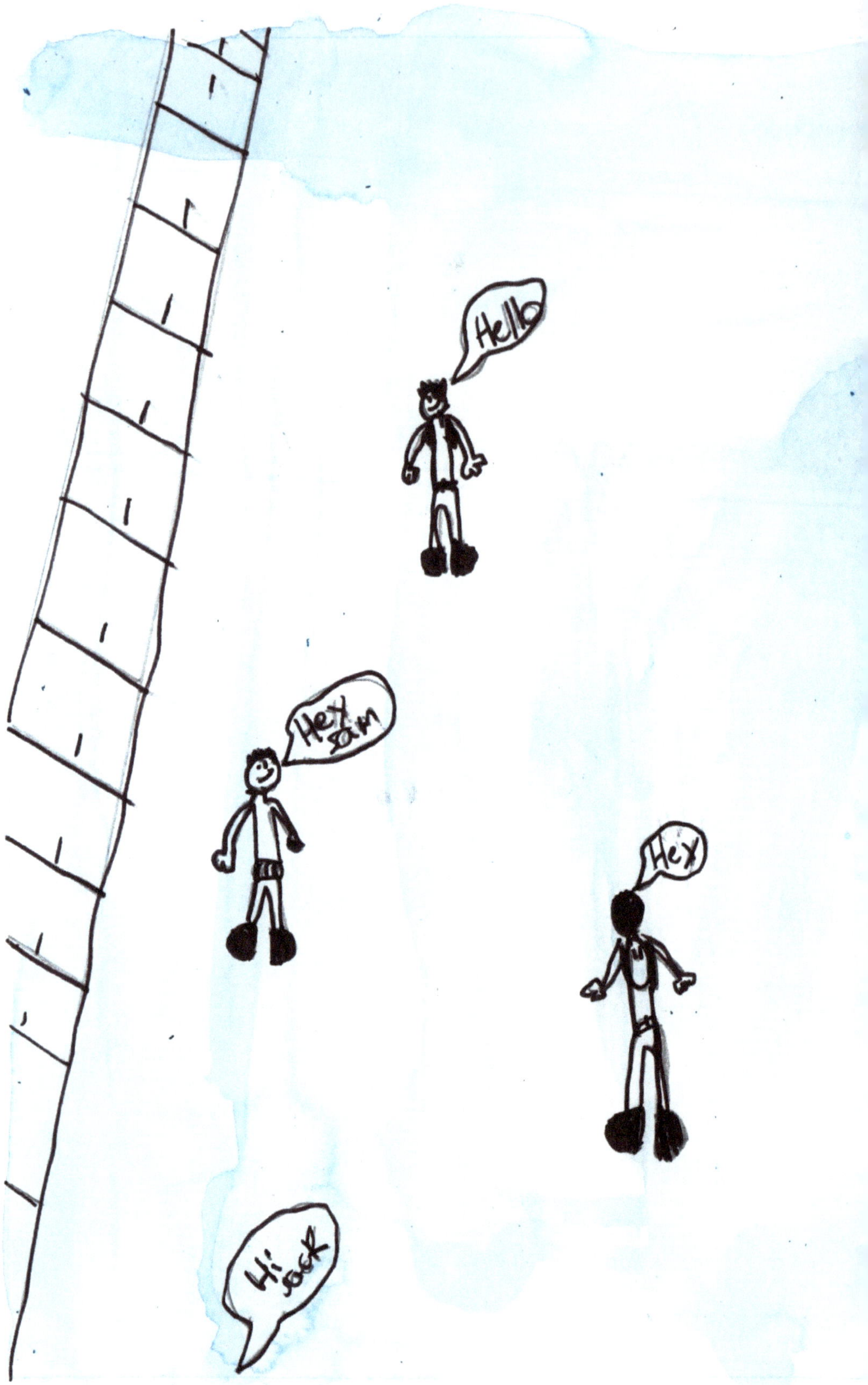

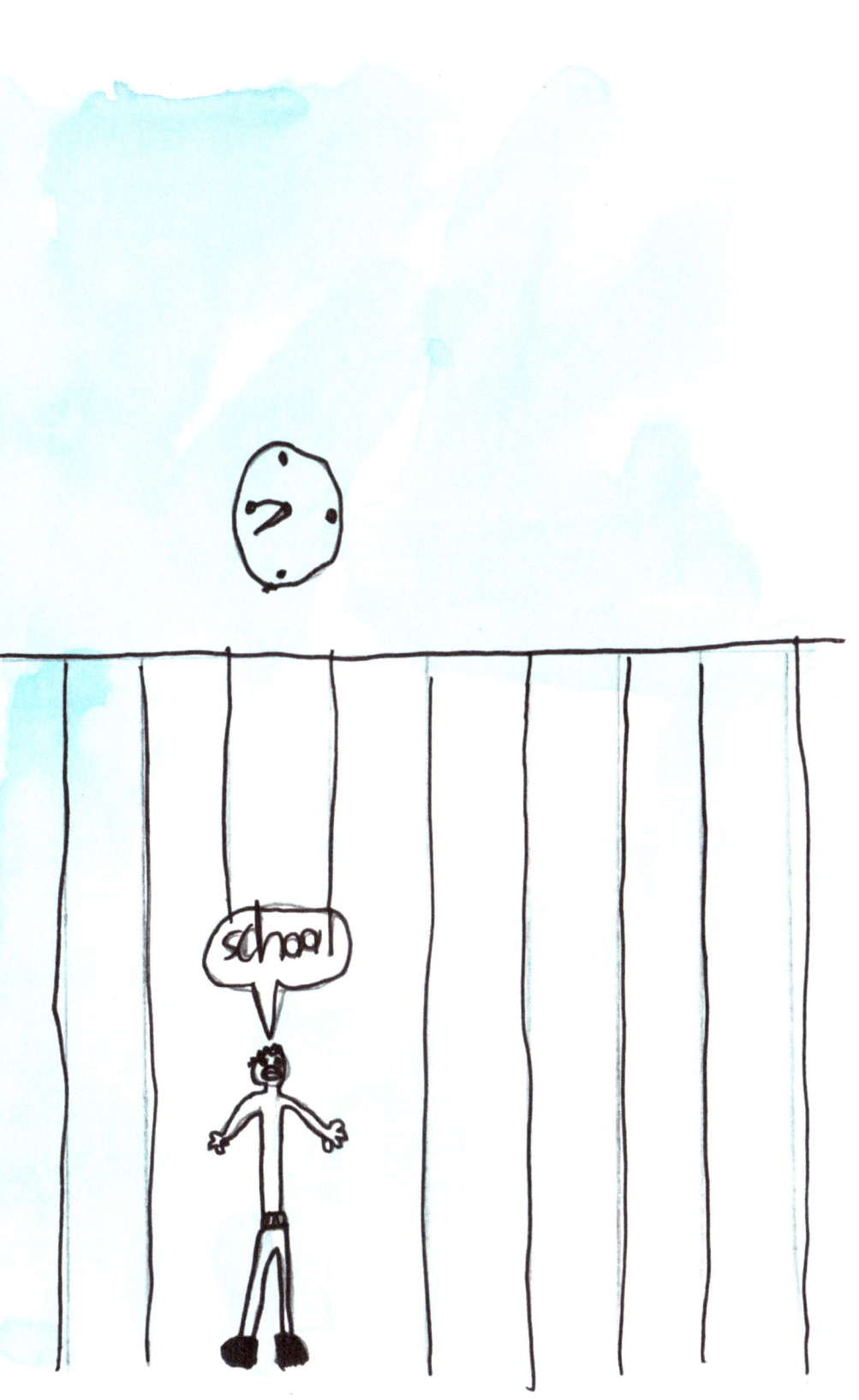

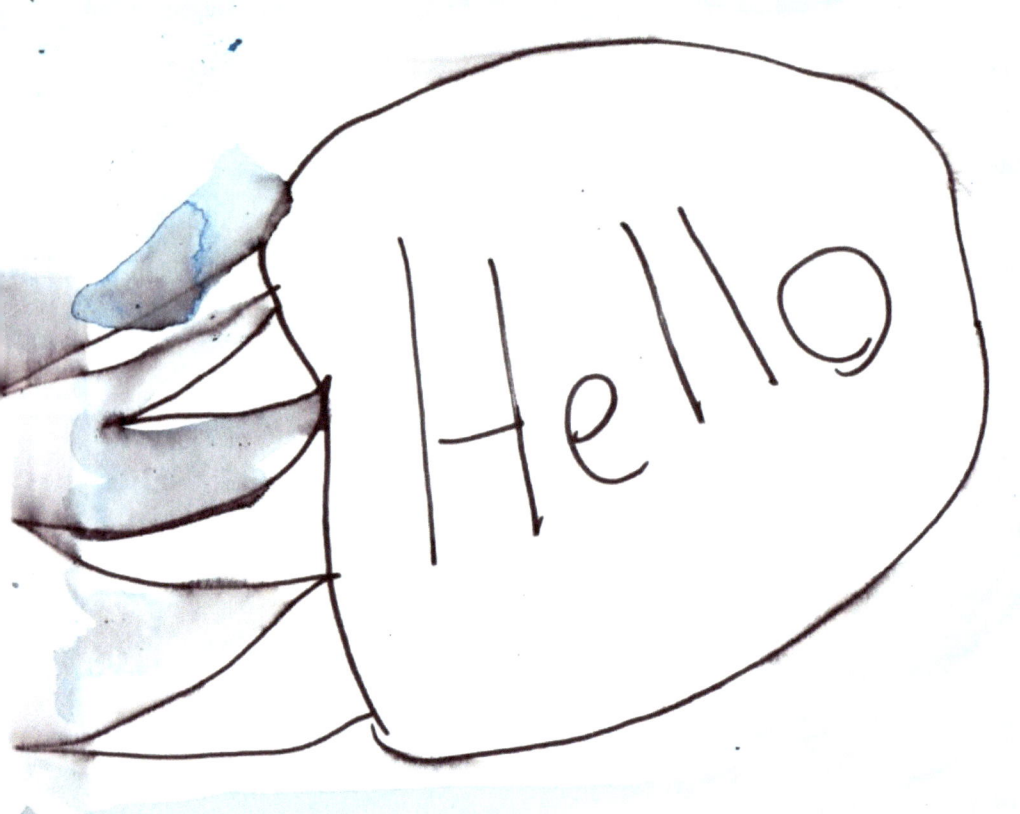

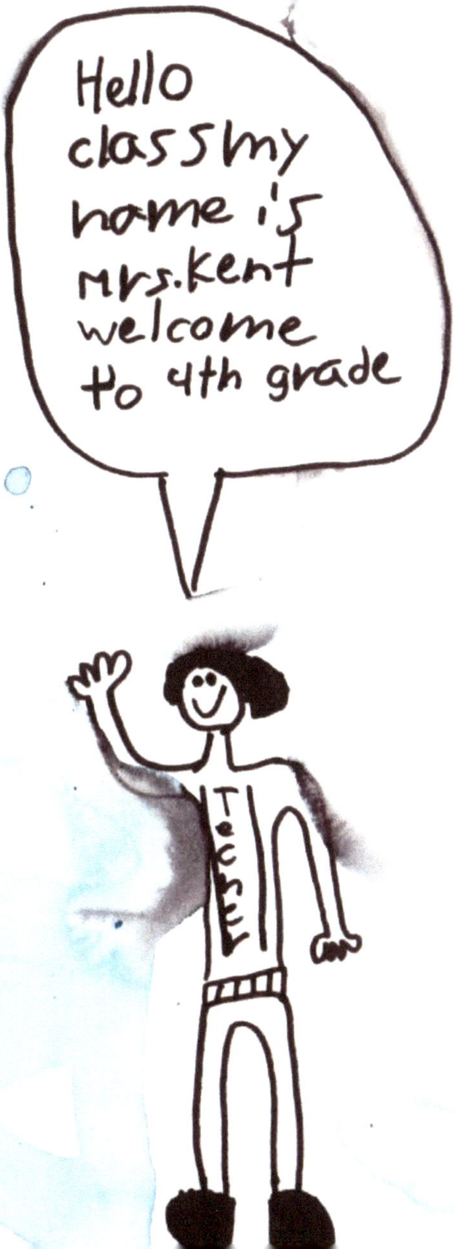
Hello class my name is mrs.kent welcome to 4th grade

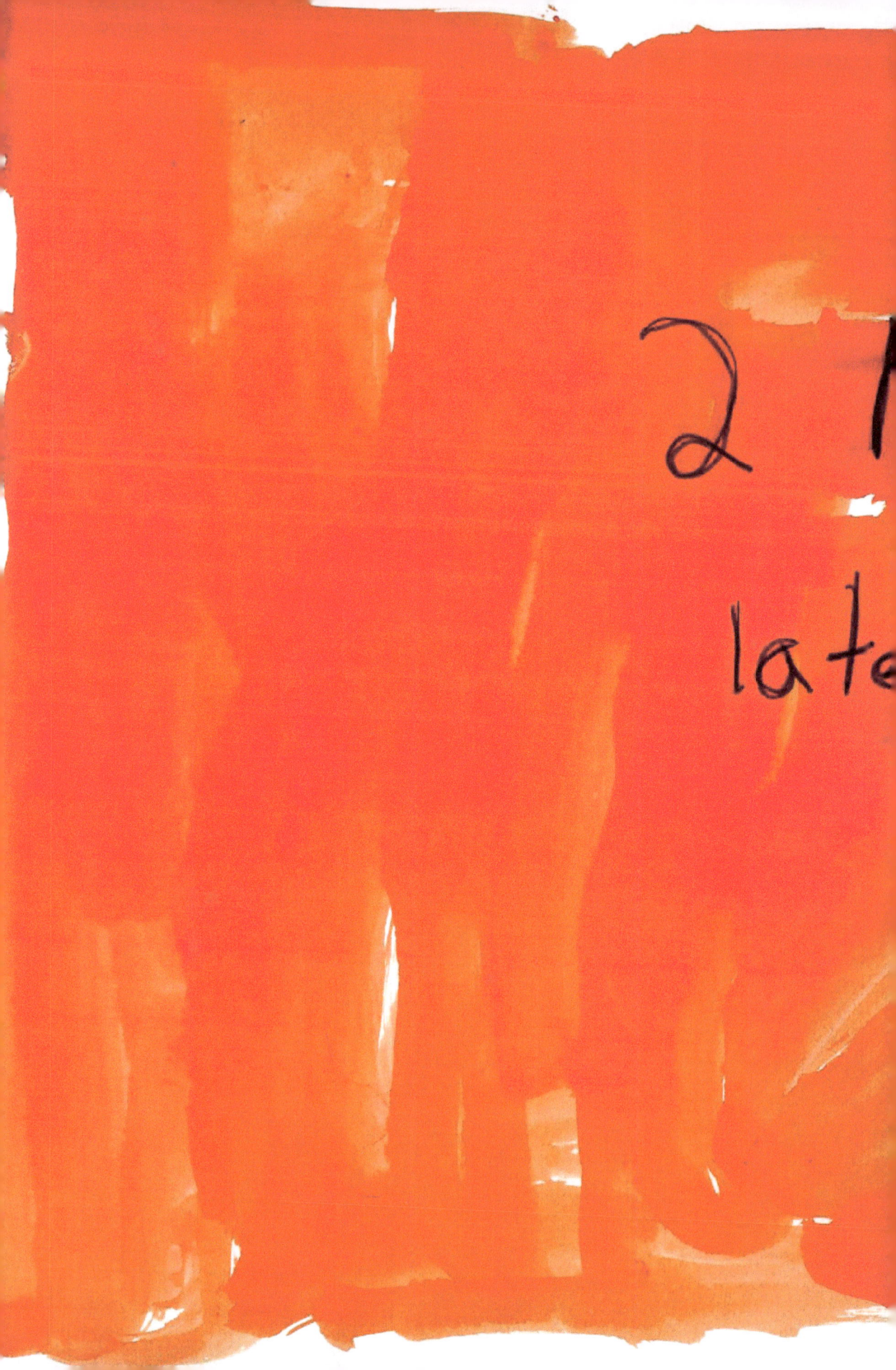

2?

late

minutes

8:47

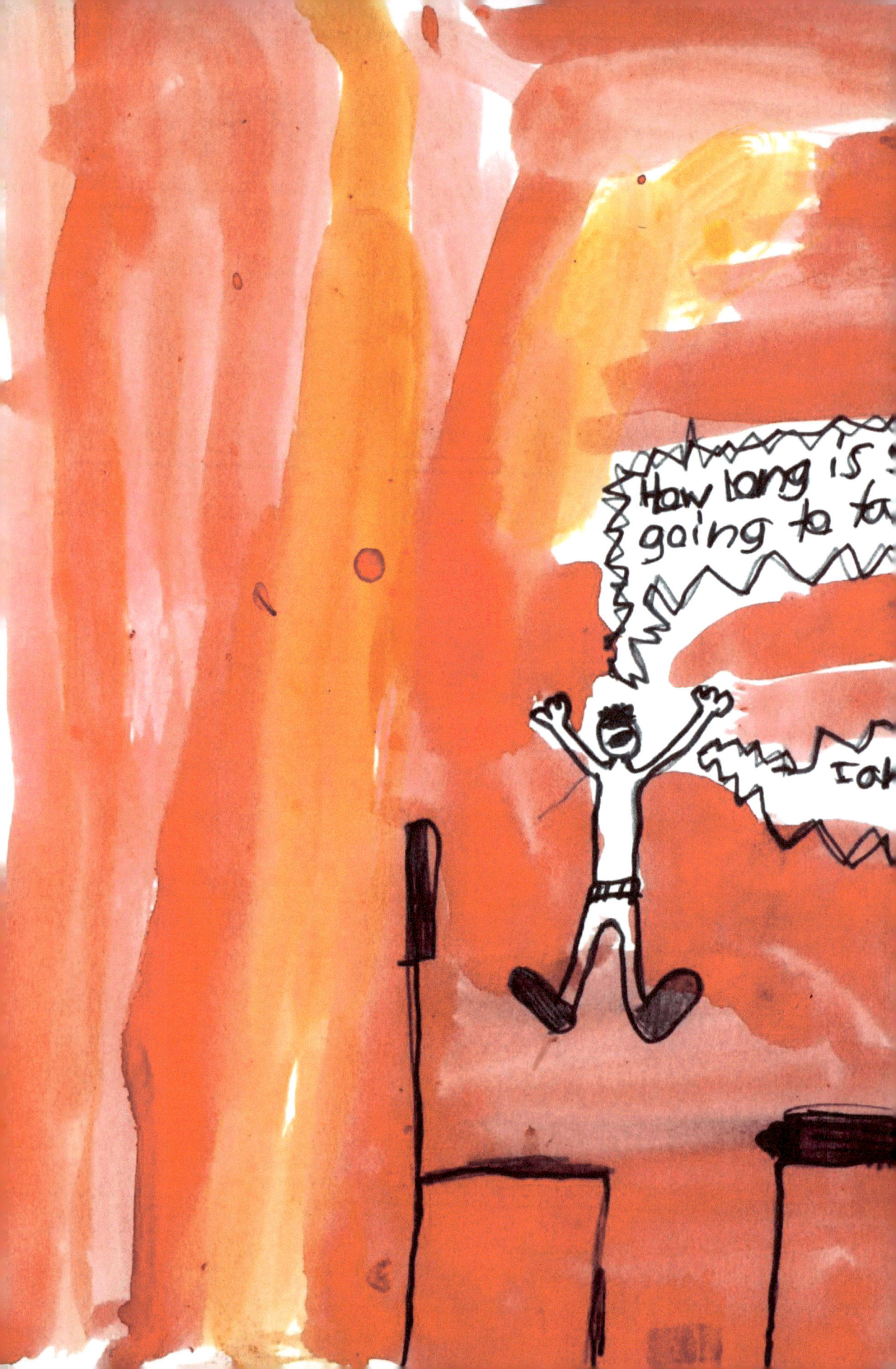

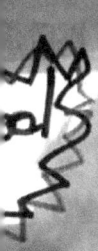

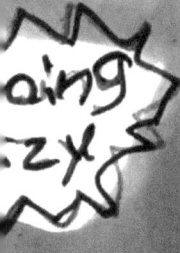

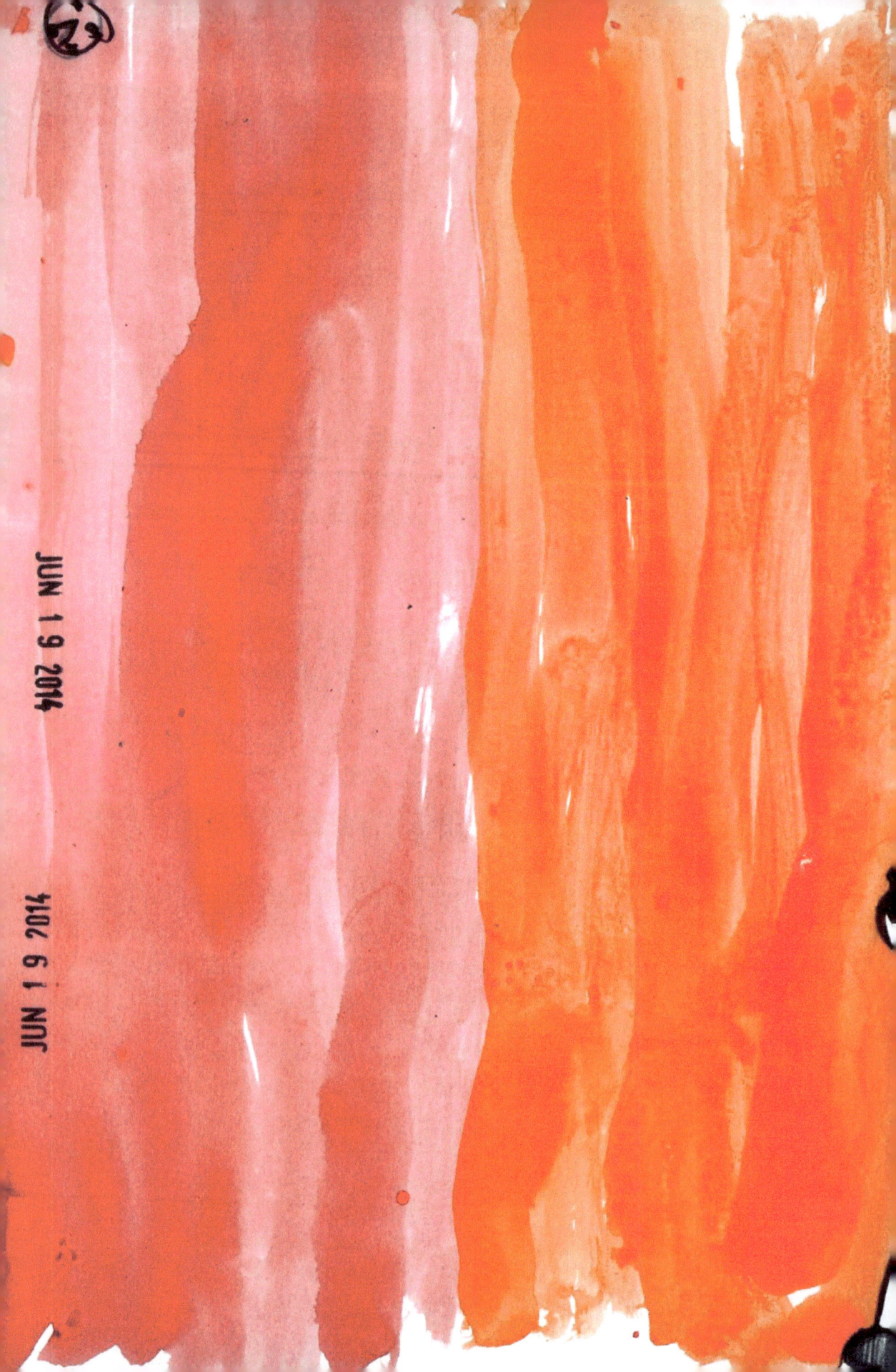

To

conten

Be

de

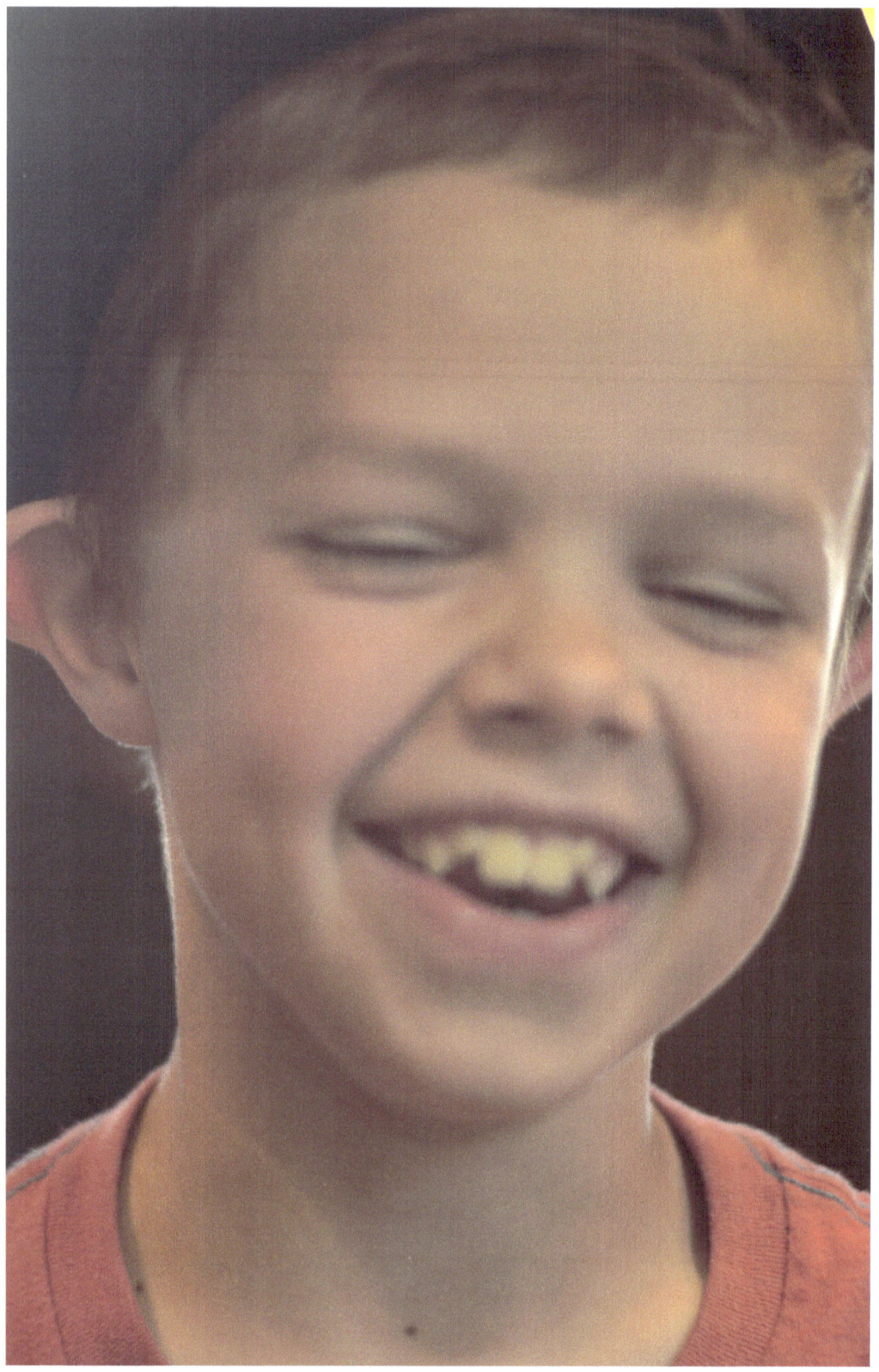

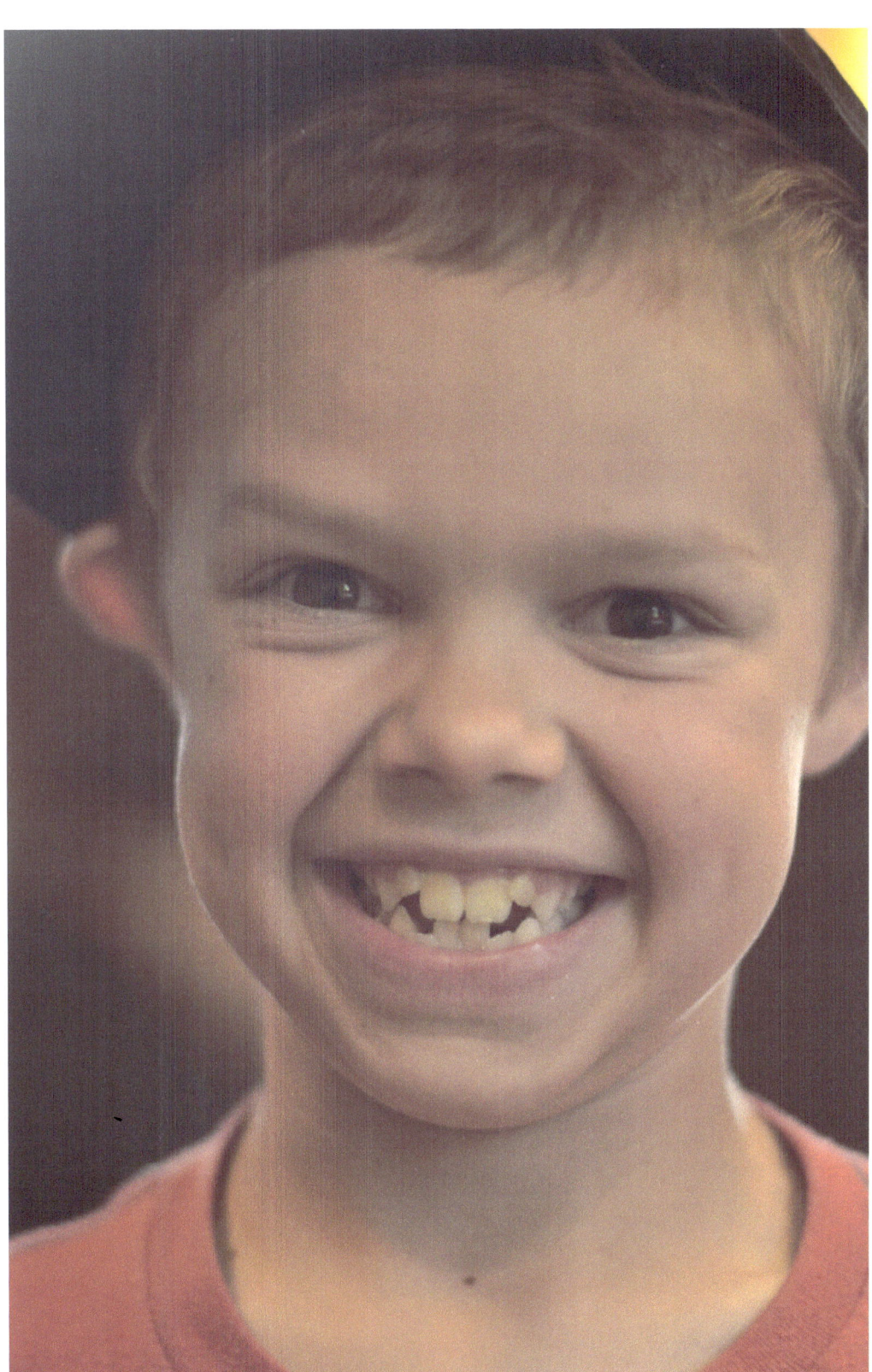

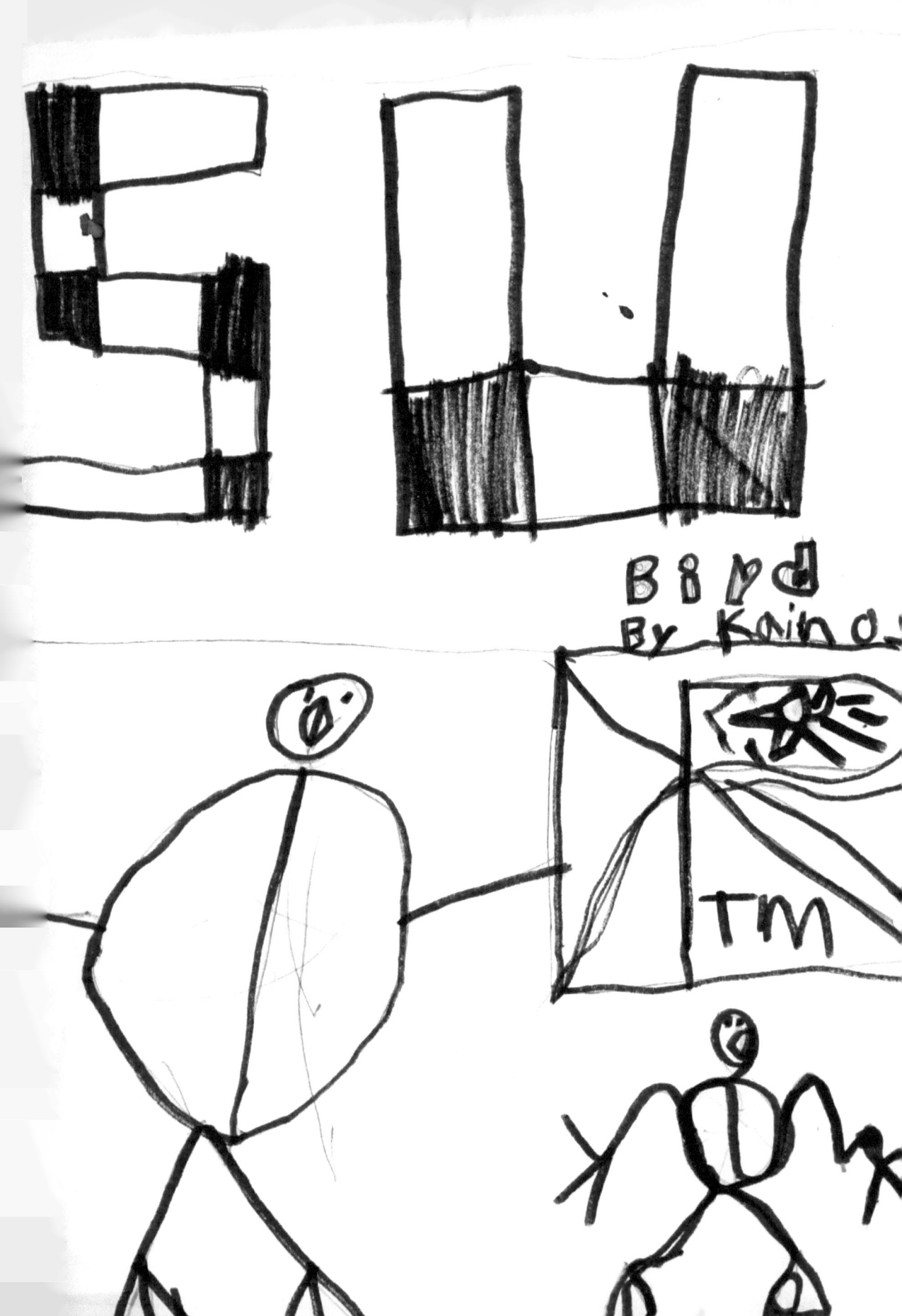

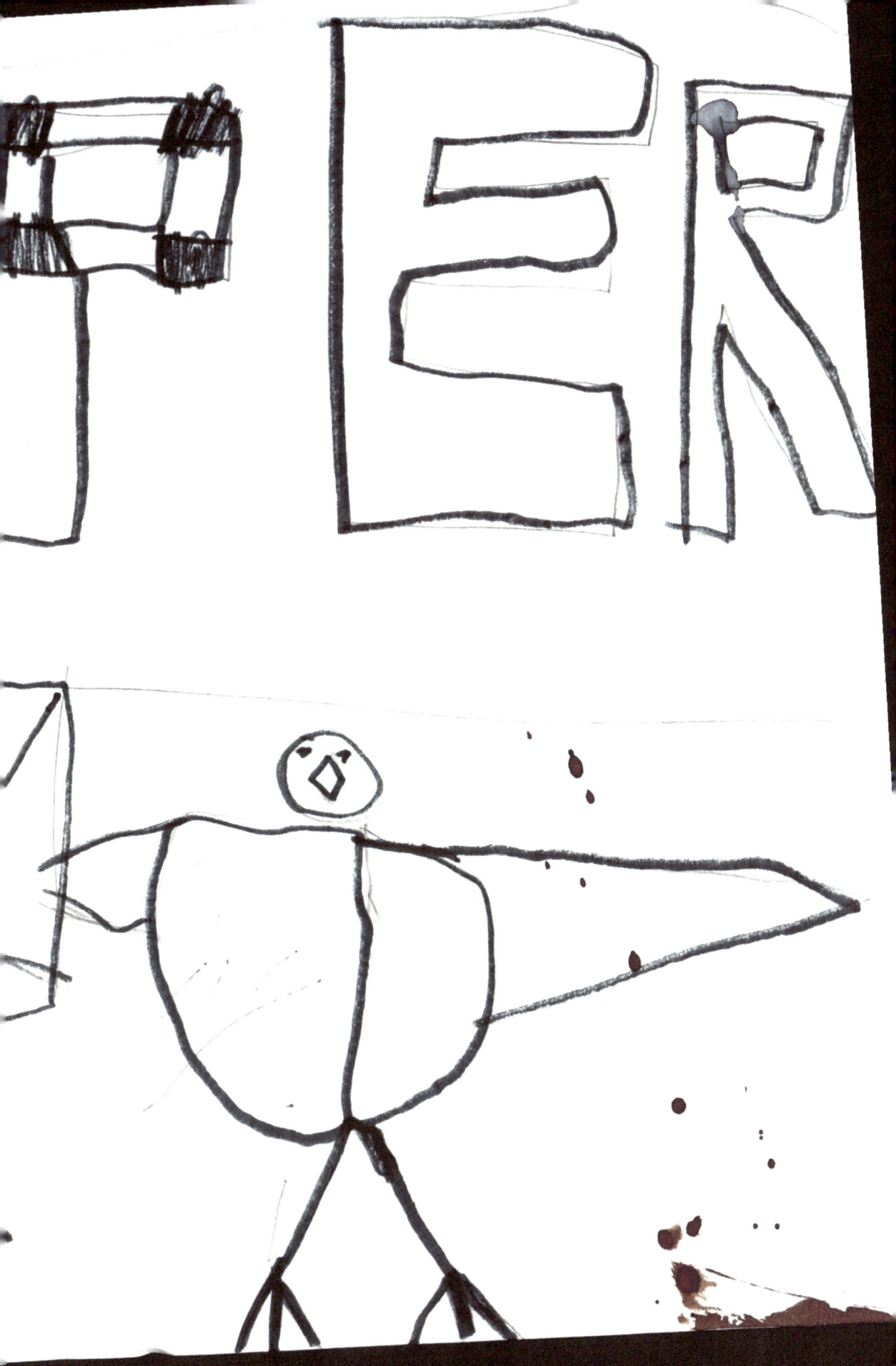

one day there was

a bird in its nest

the tree got on

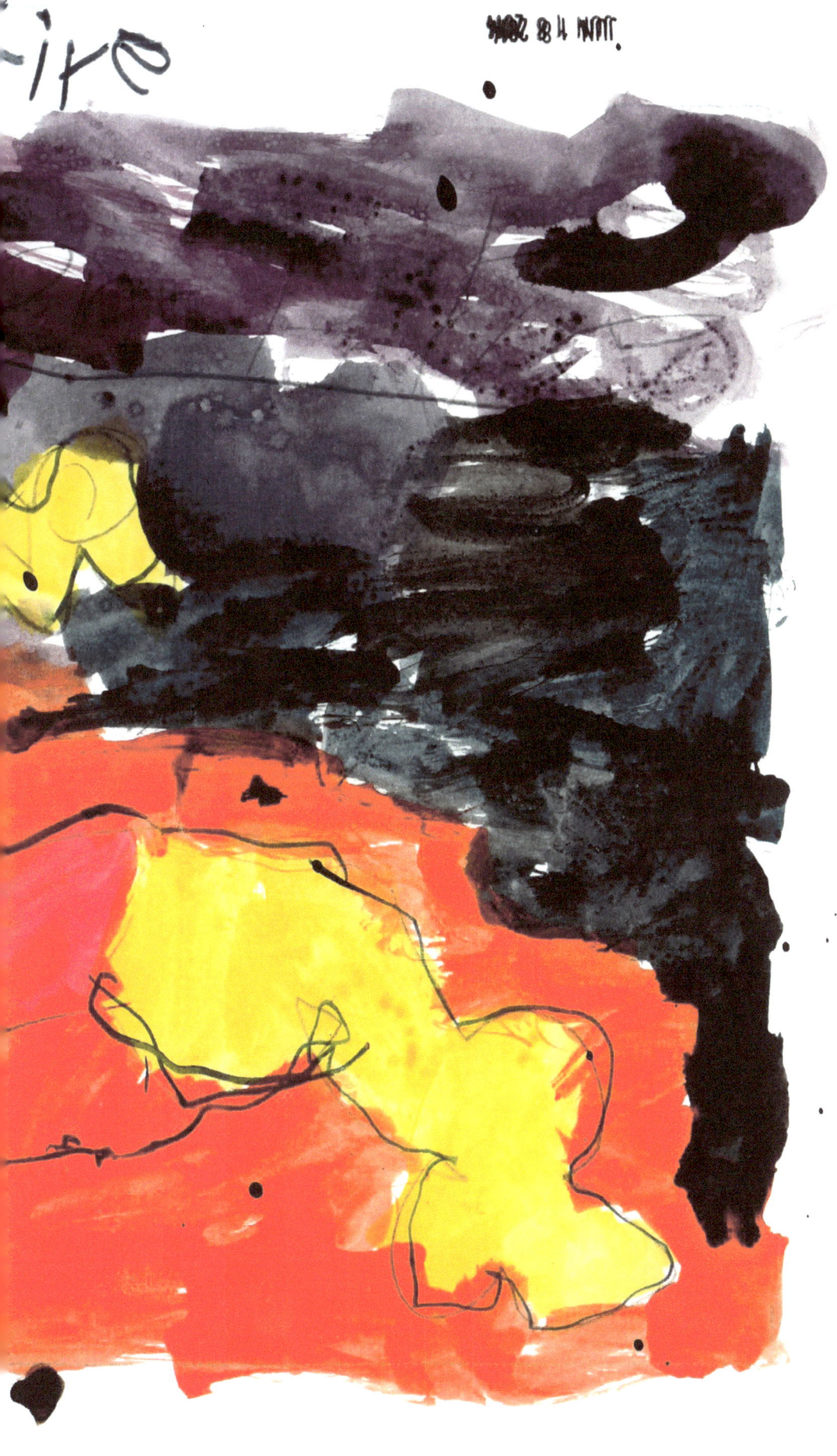

the bird walk

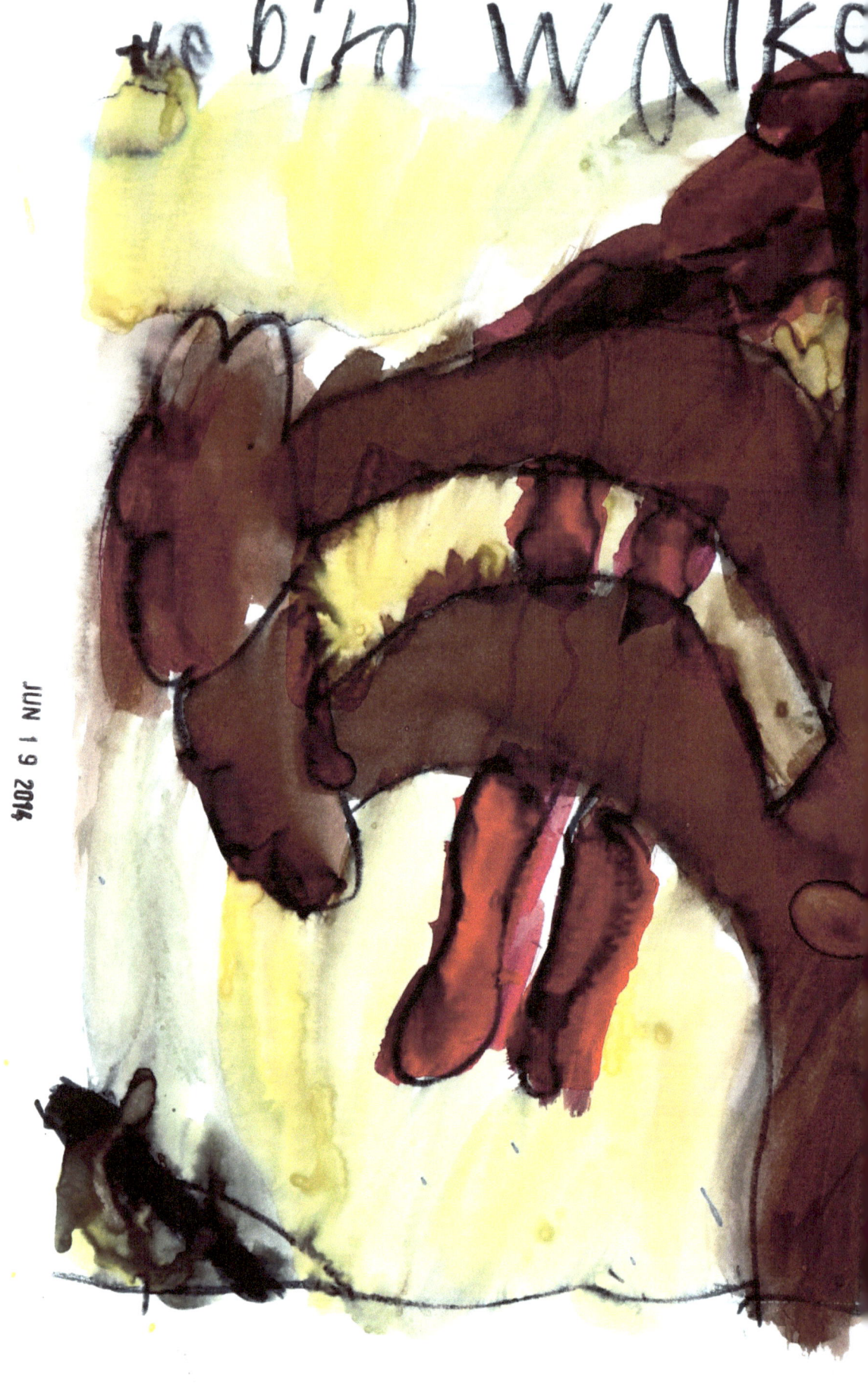

away

to be

tina

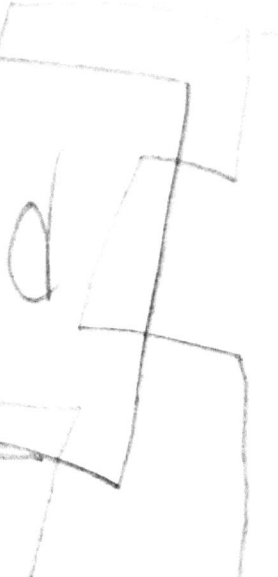

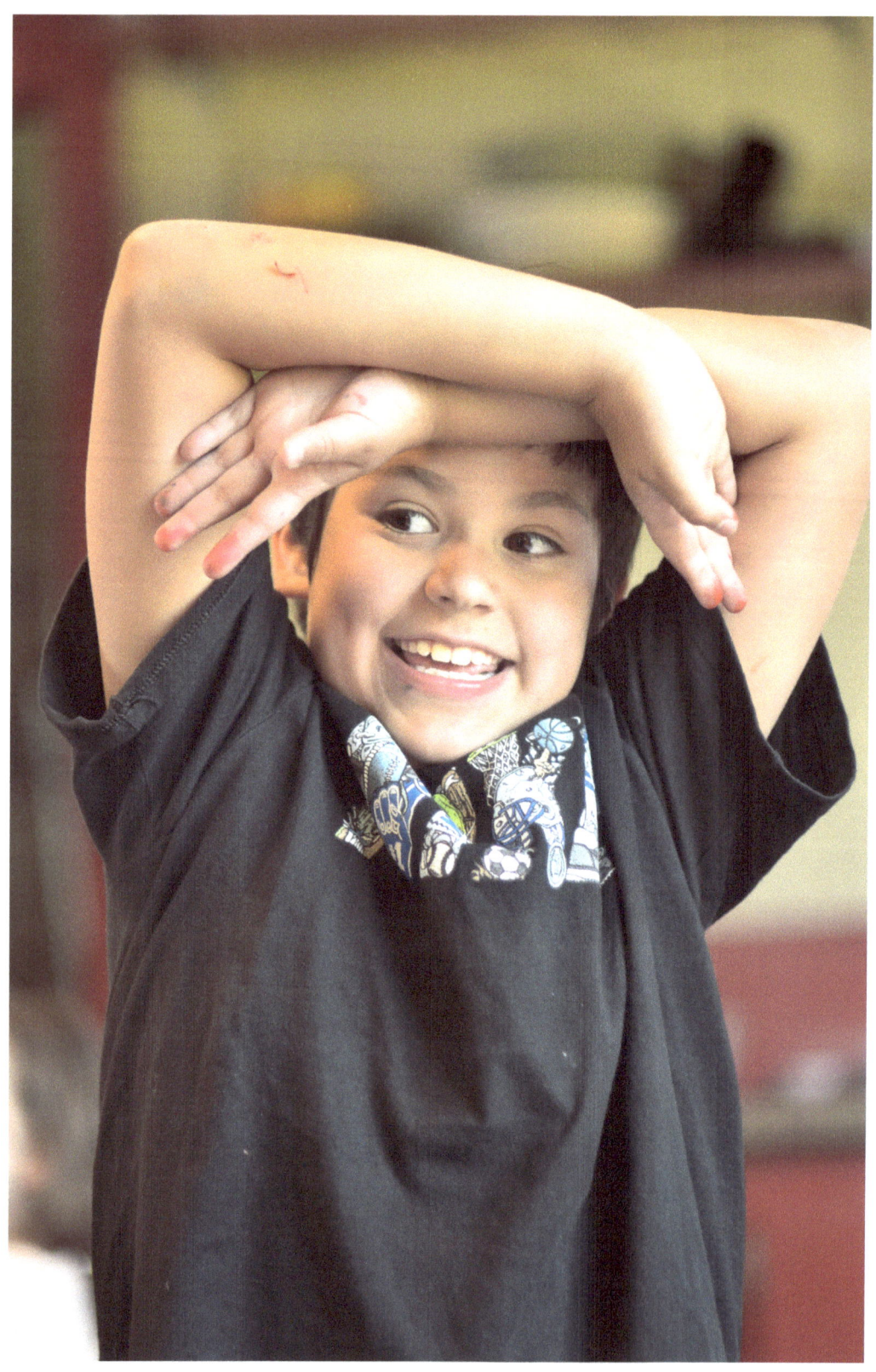

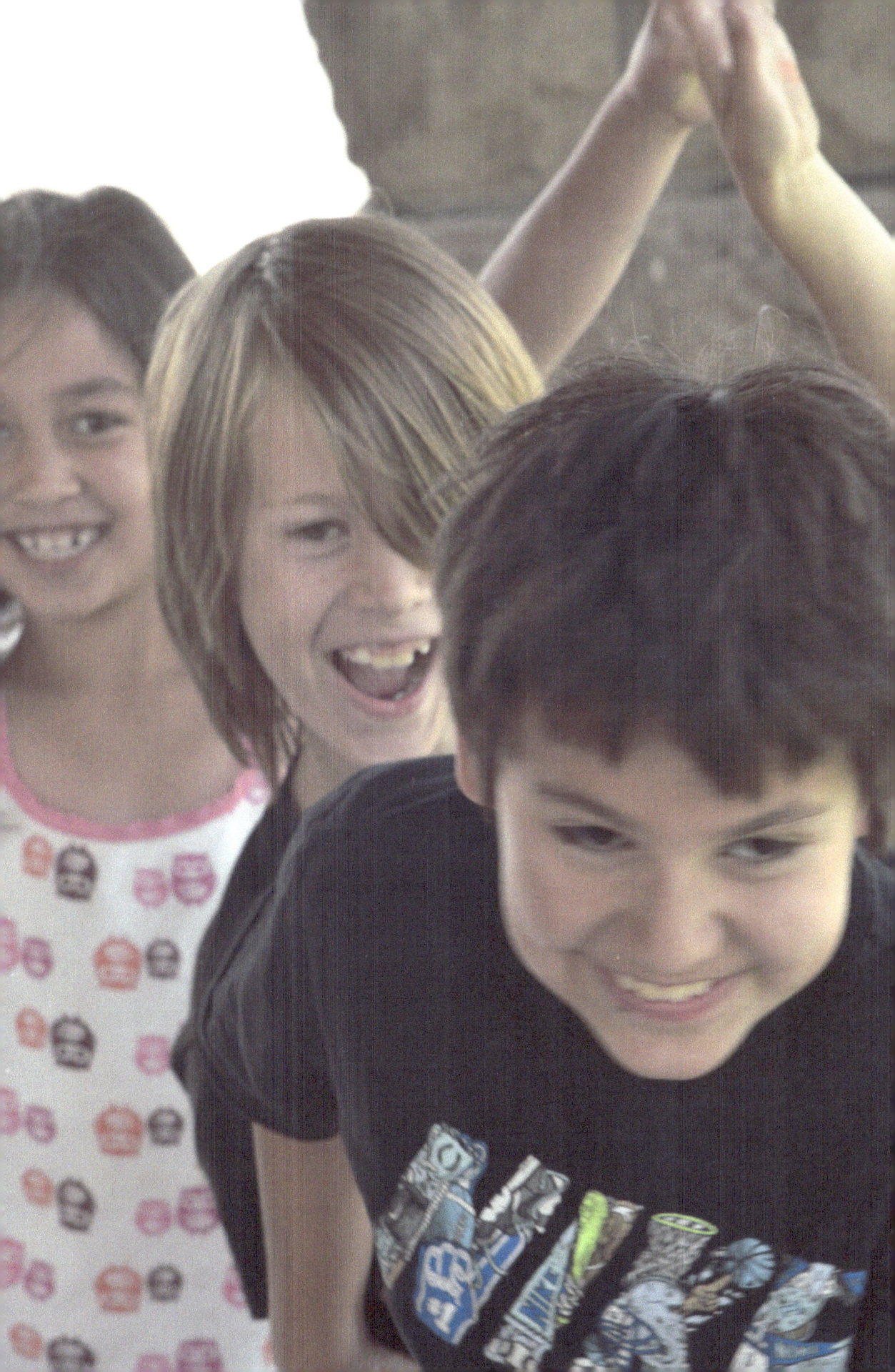

the free

the free S...

D

BY: Gabe Mill...

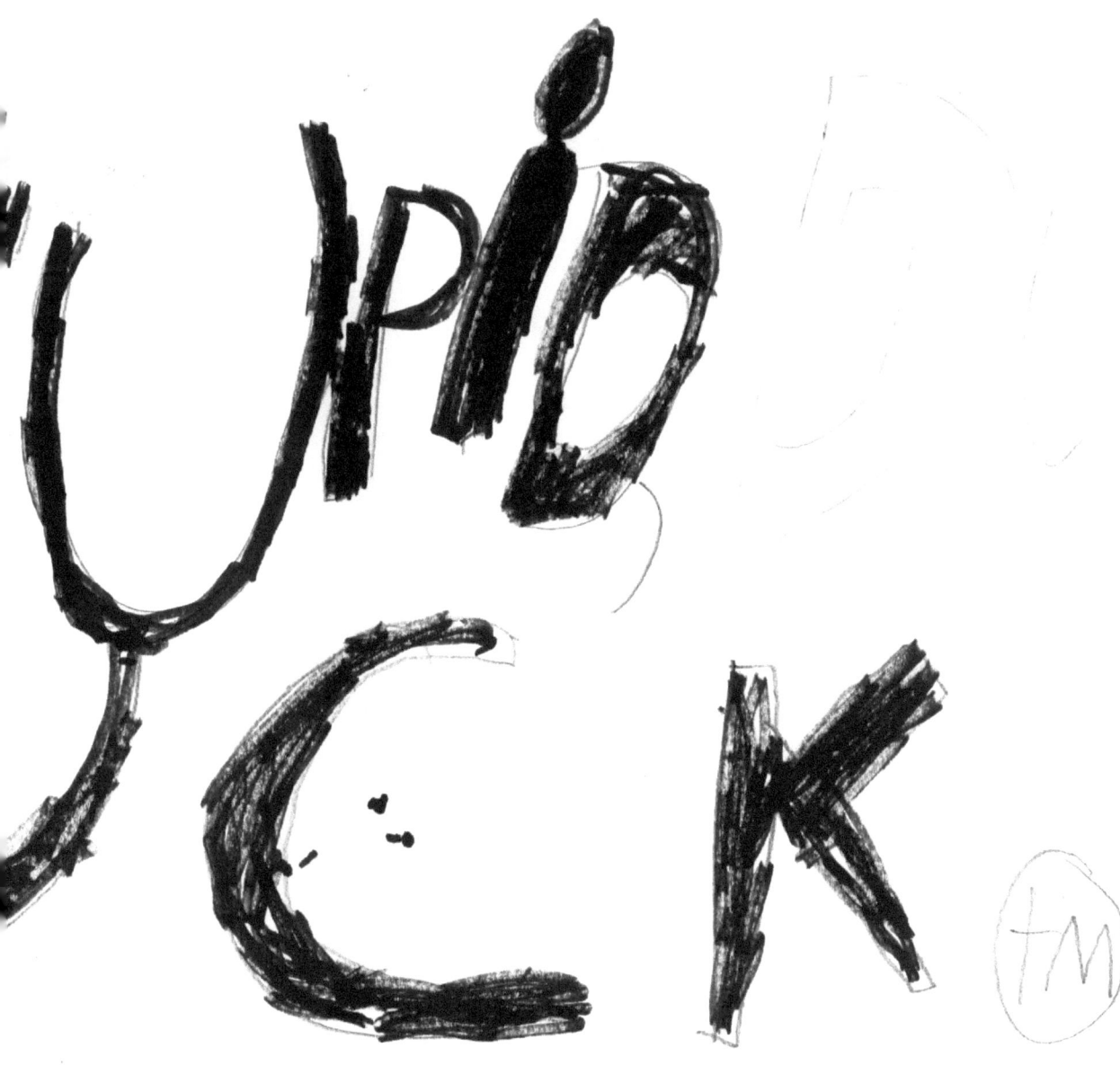

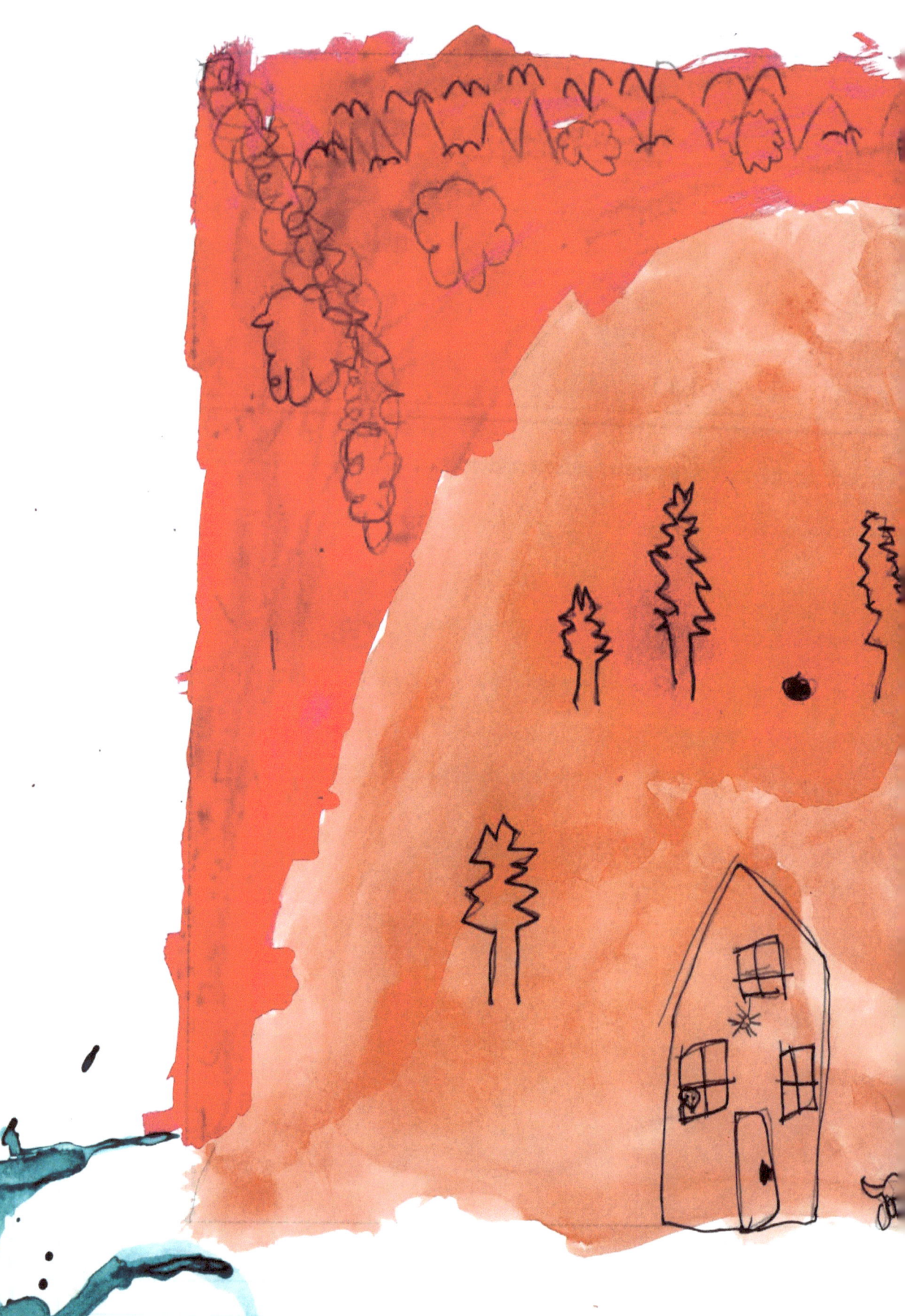

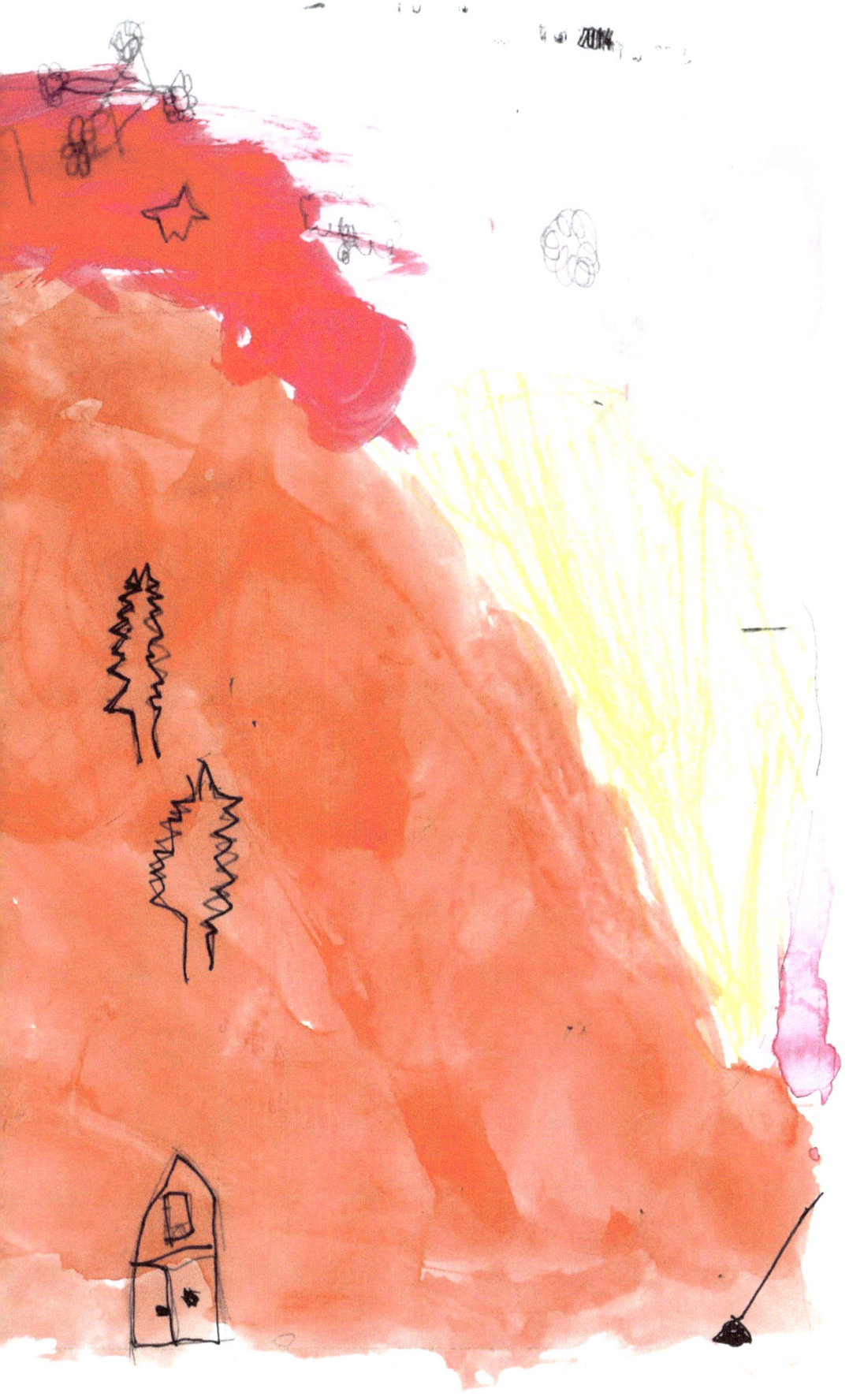

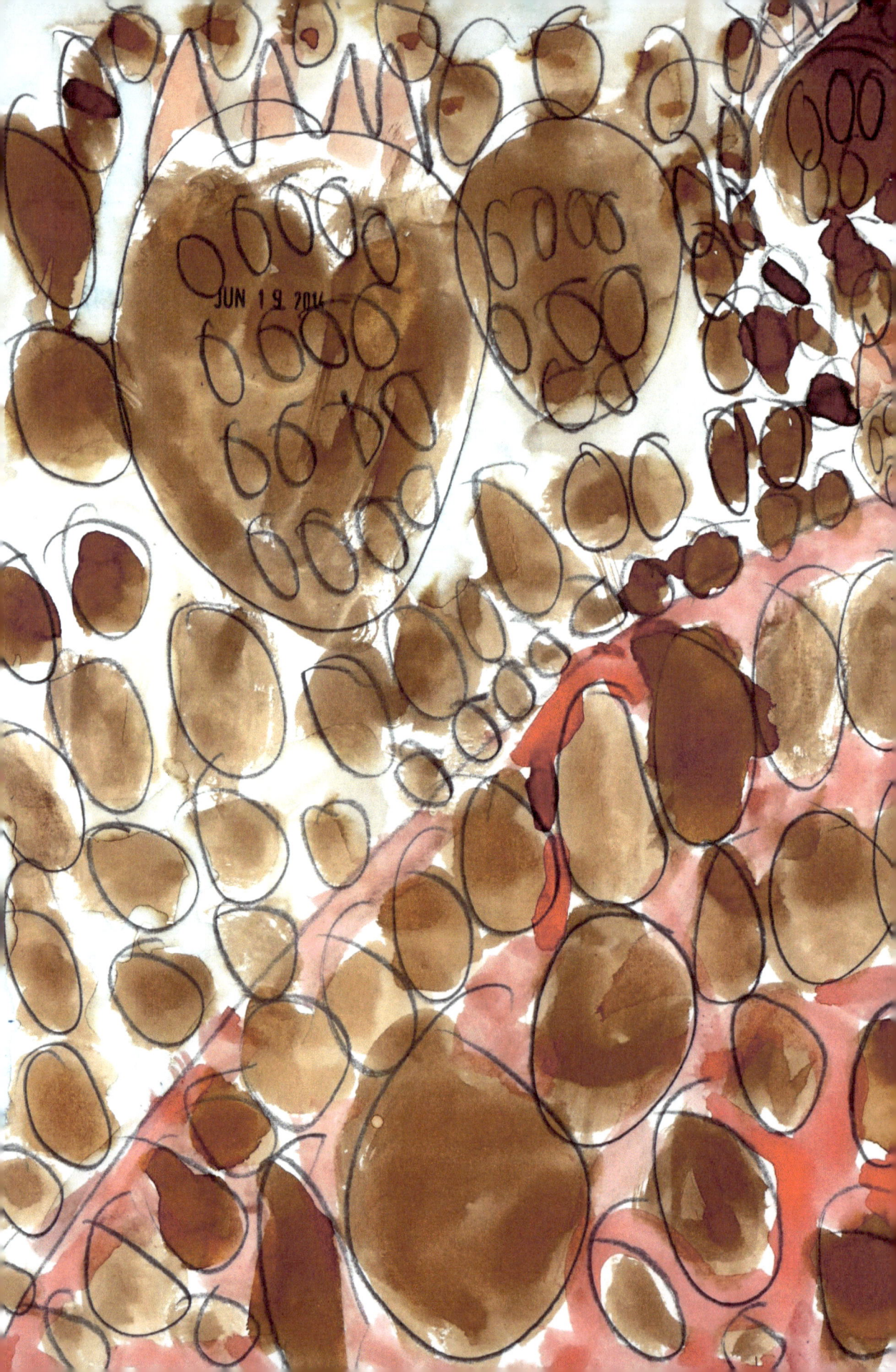

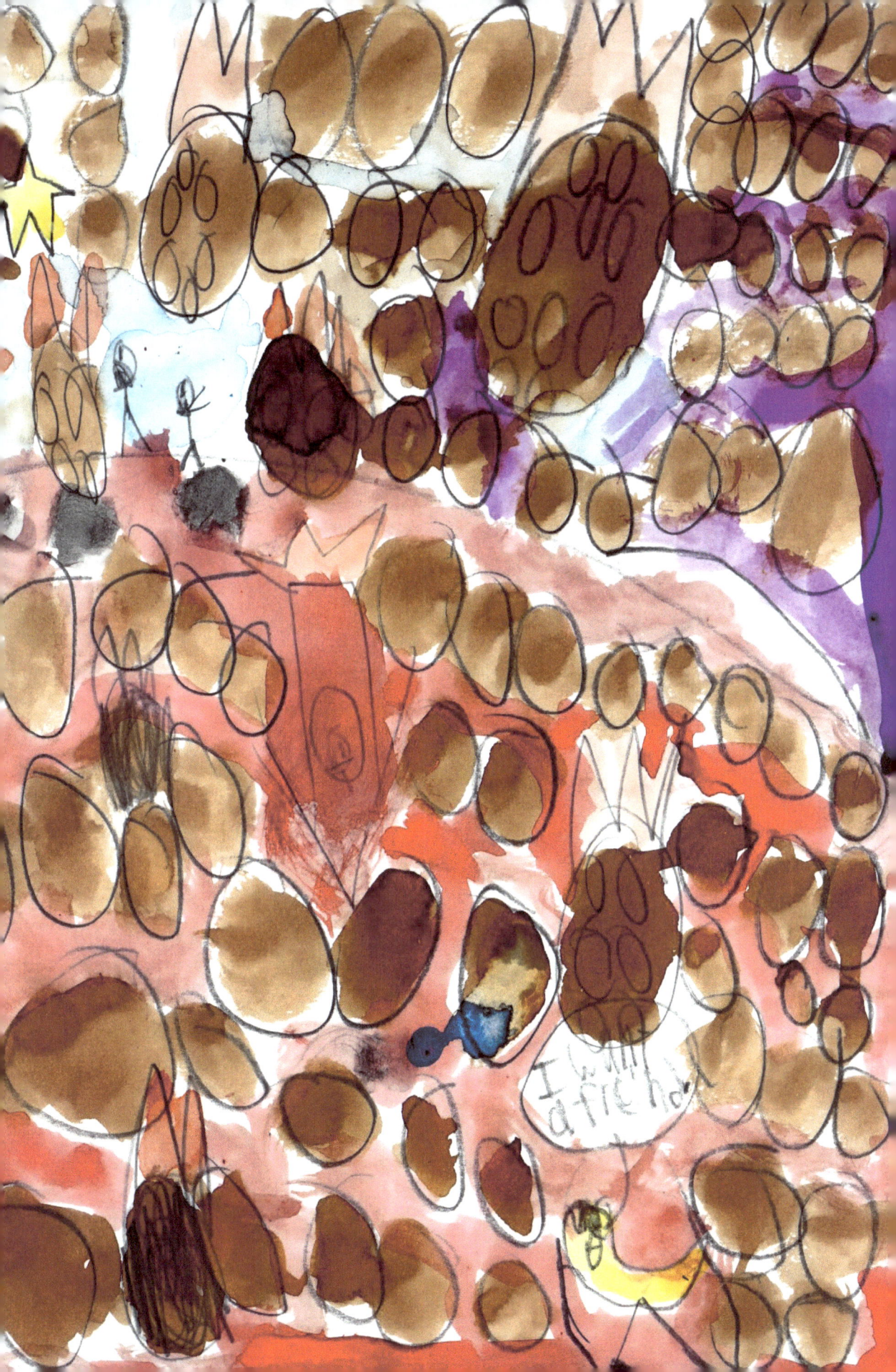

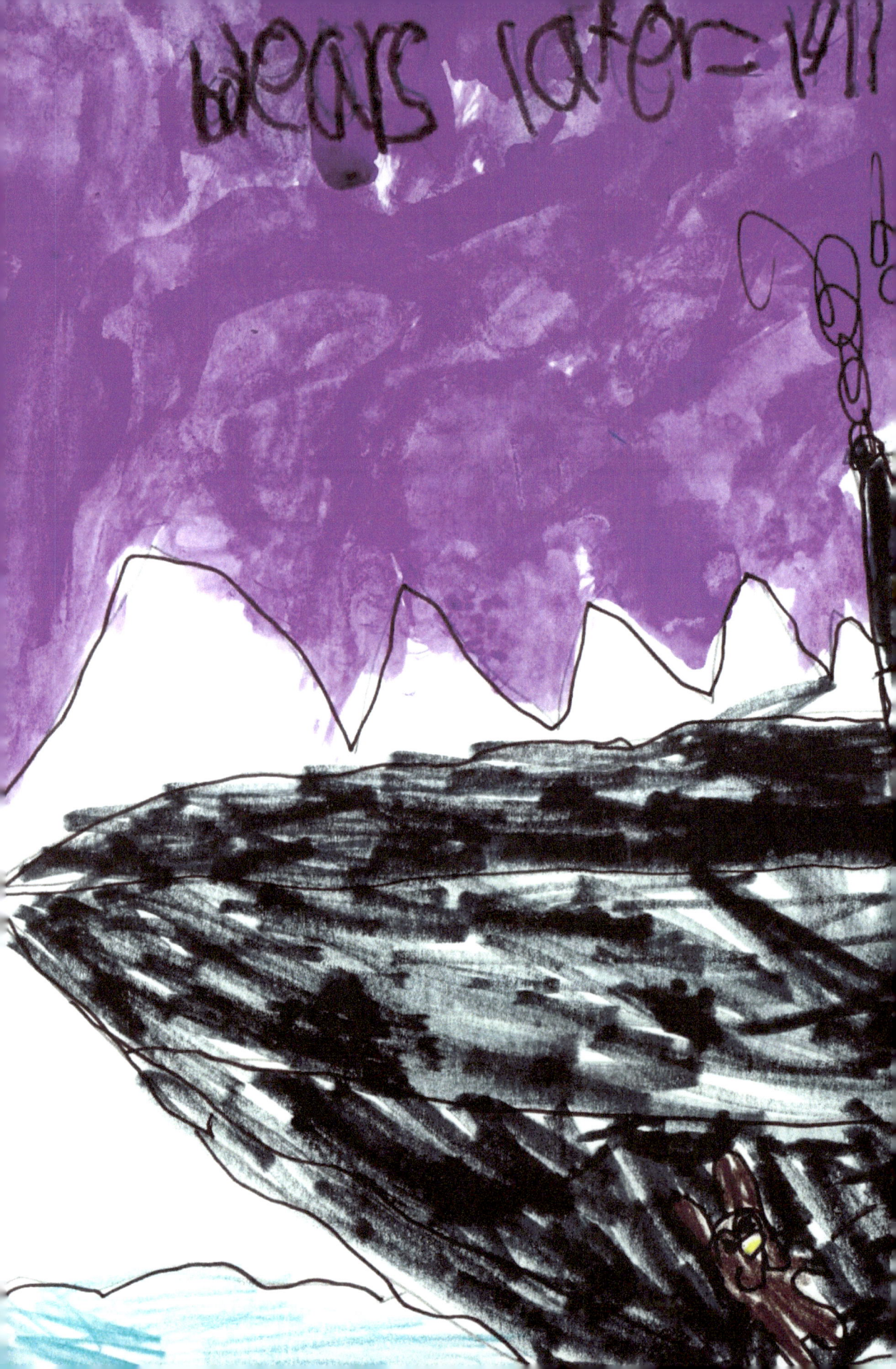

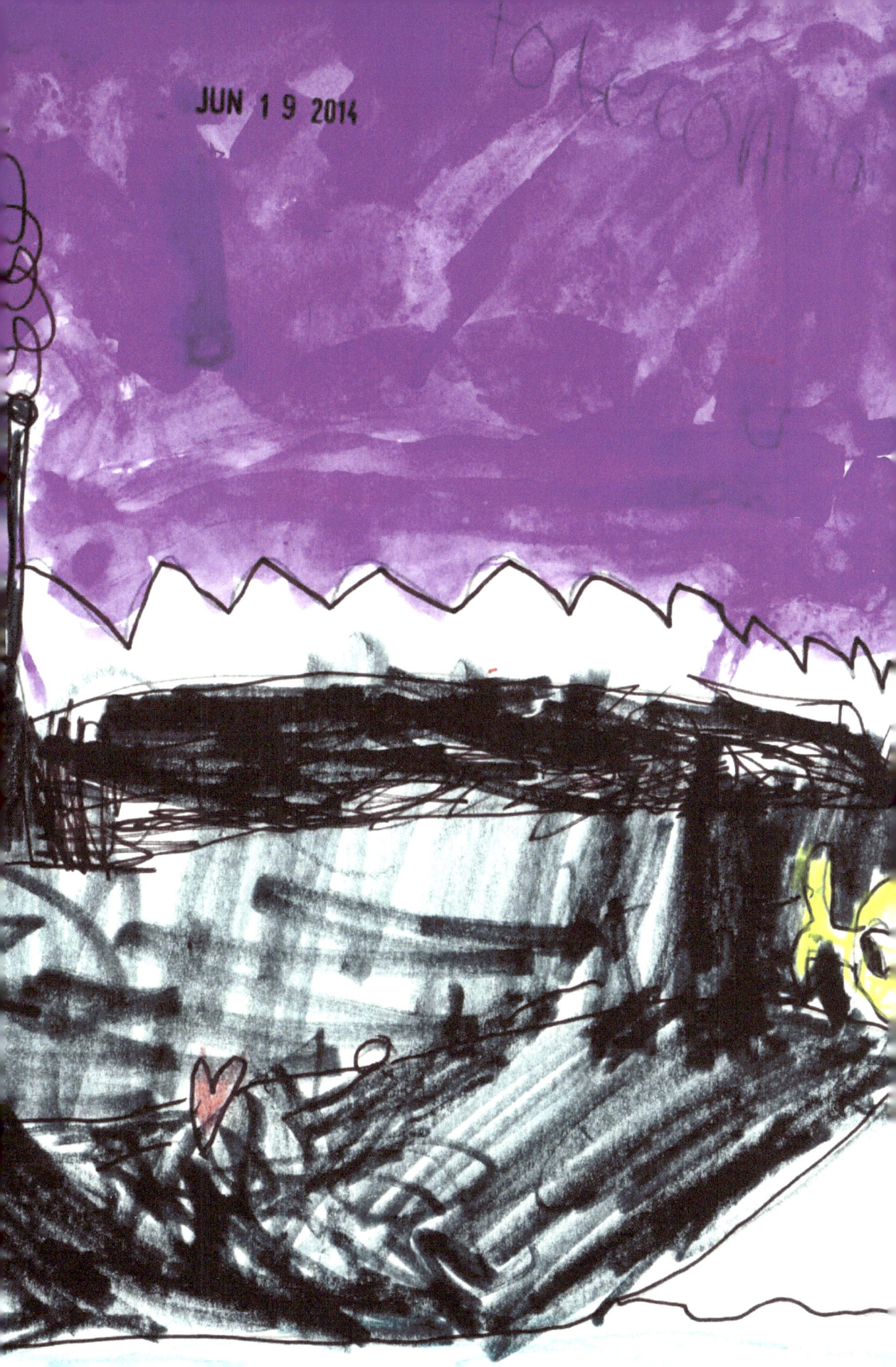

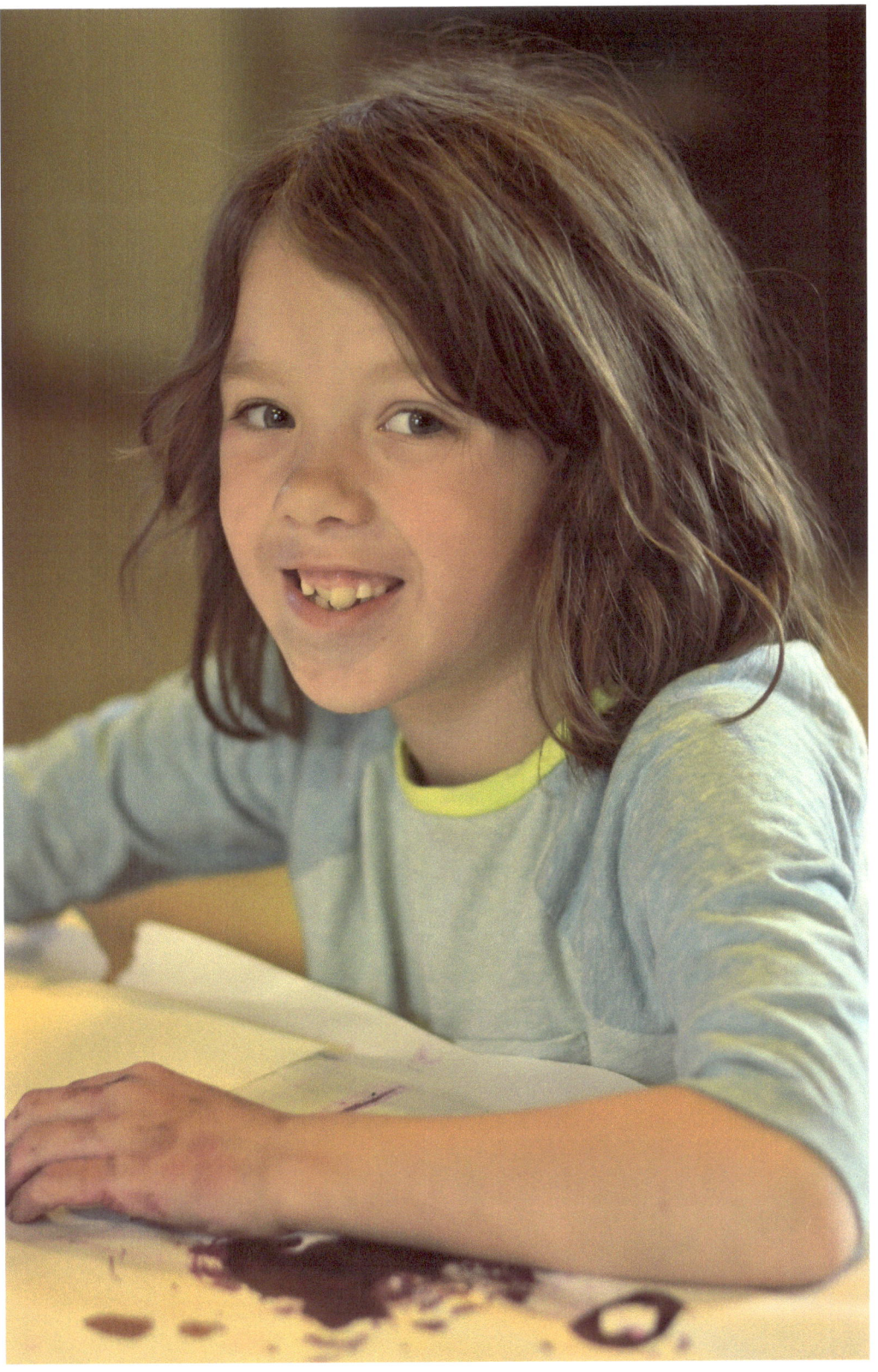

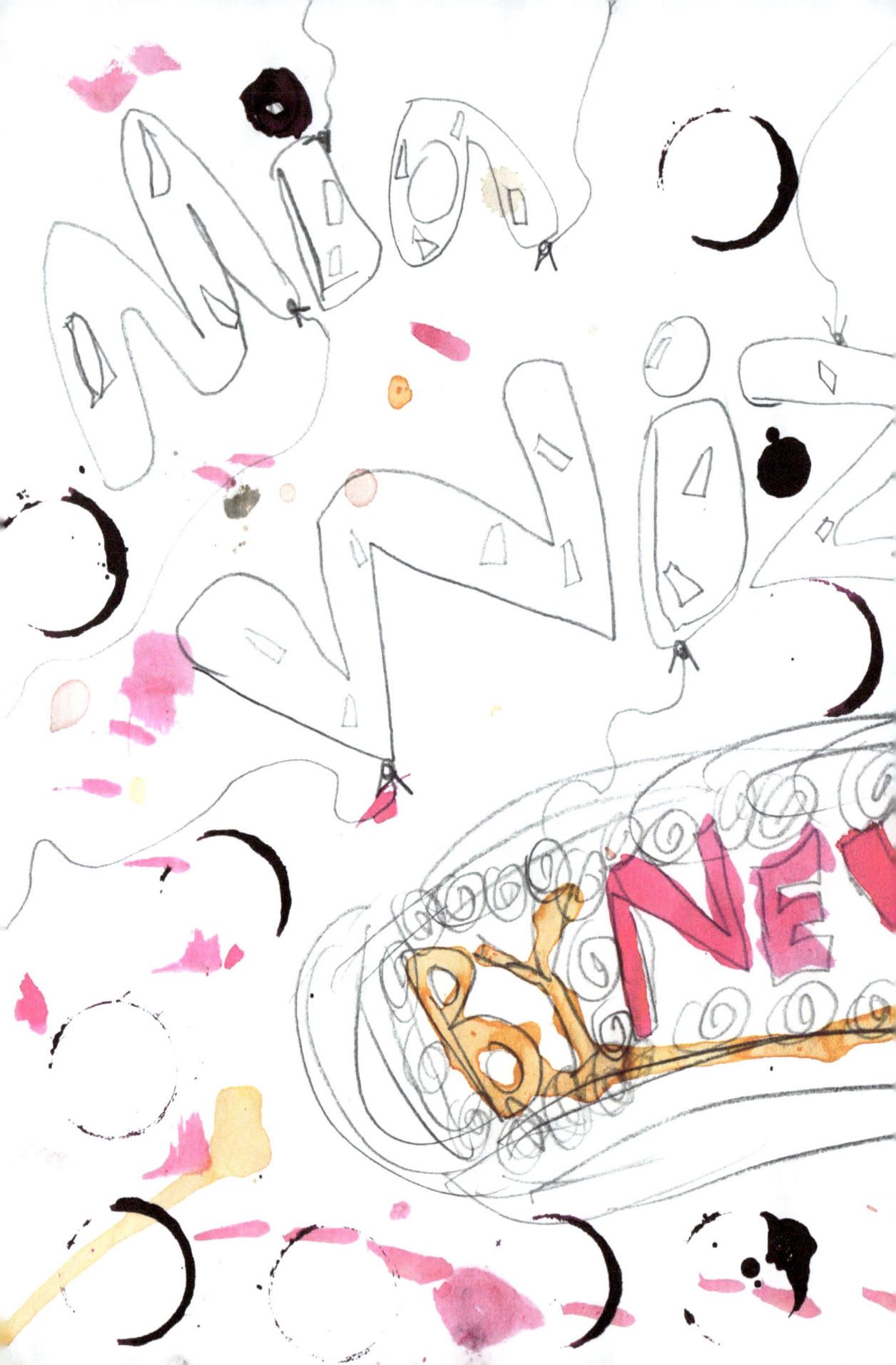

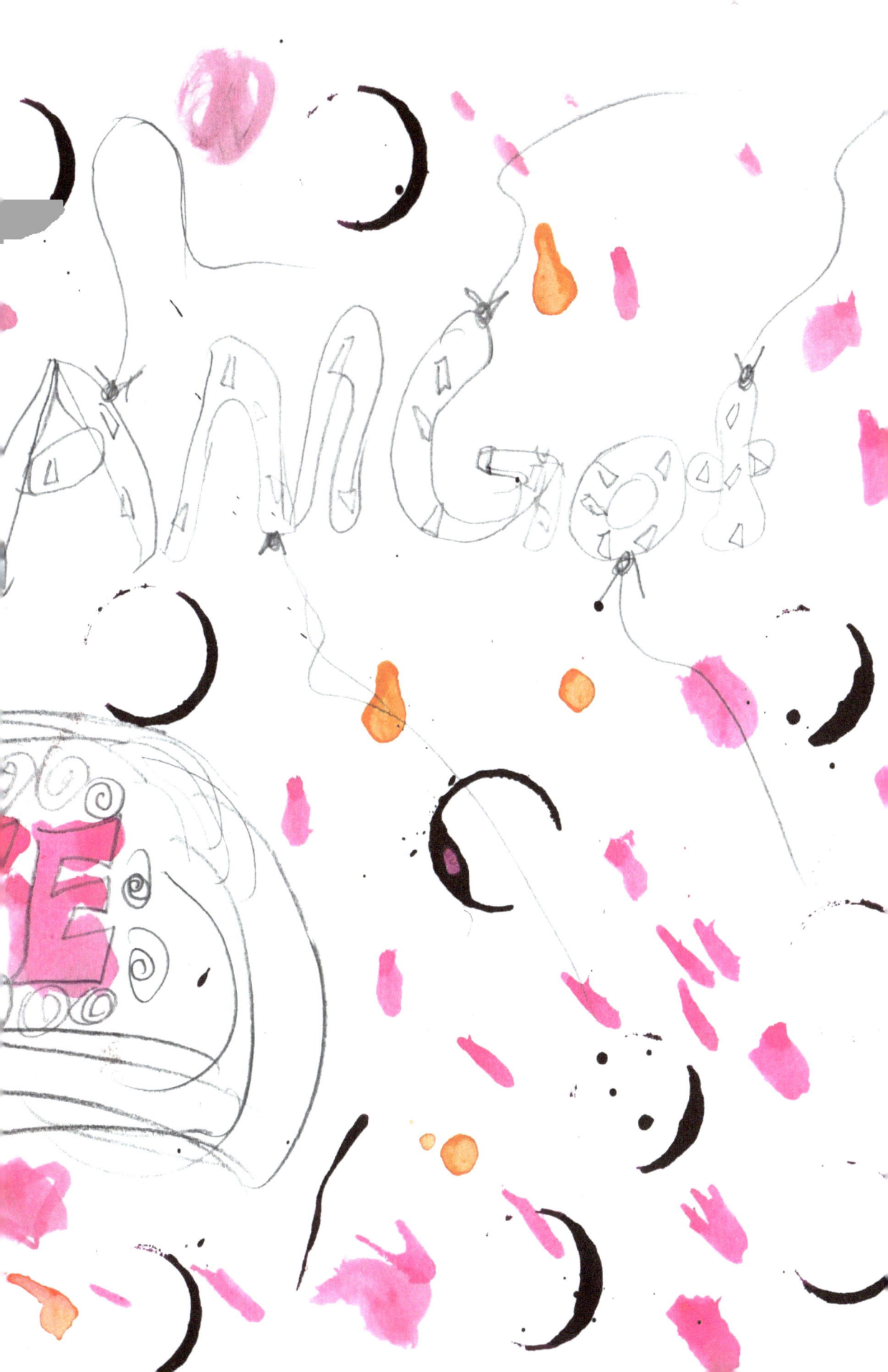

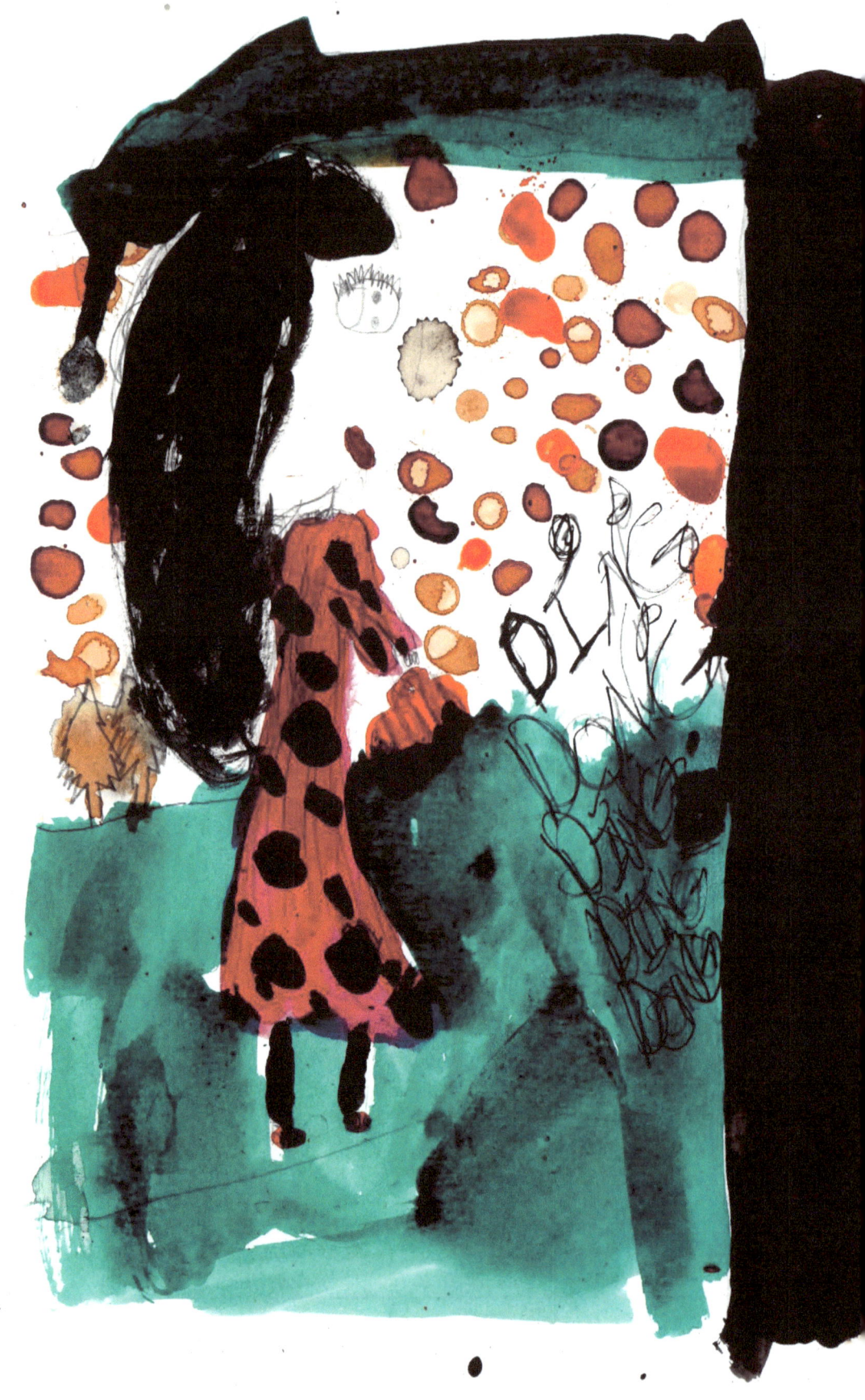

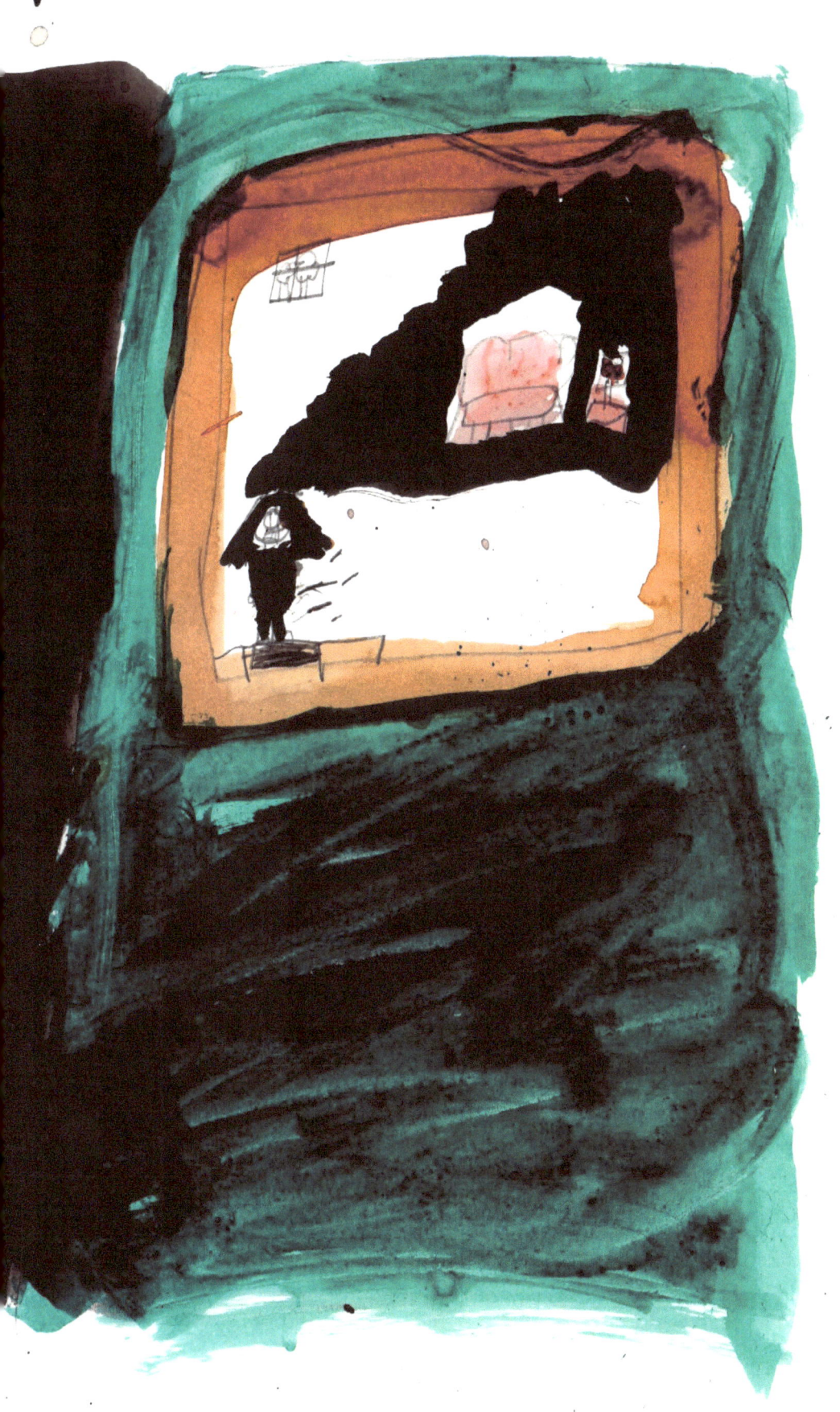

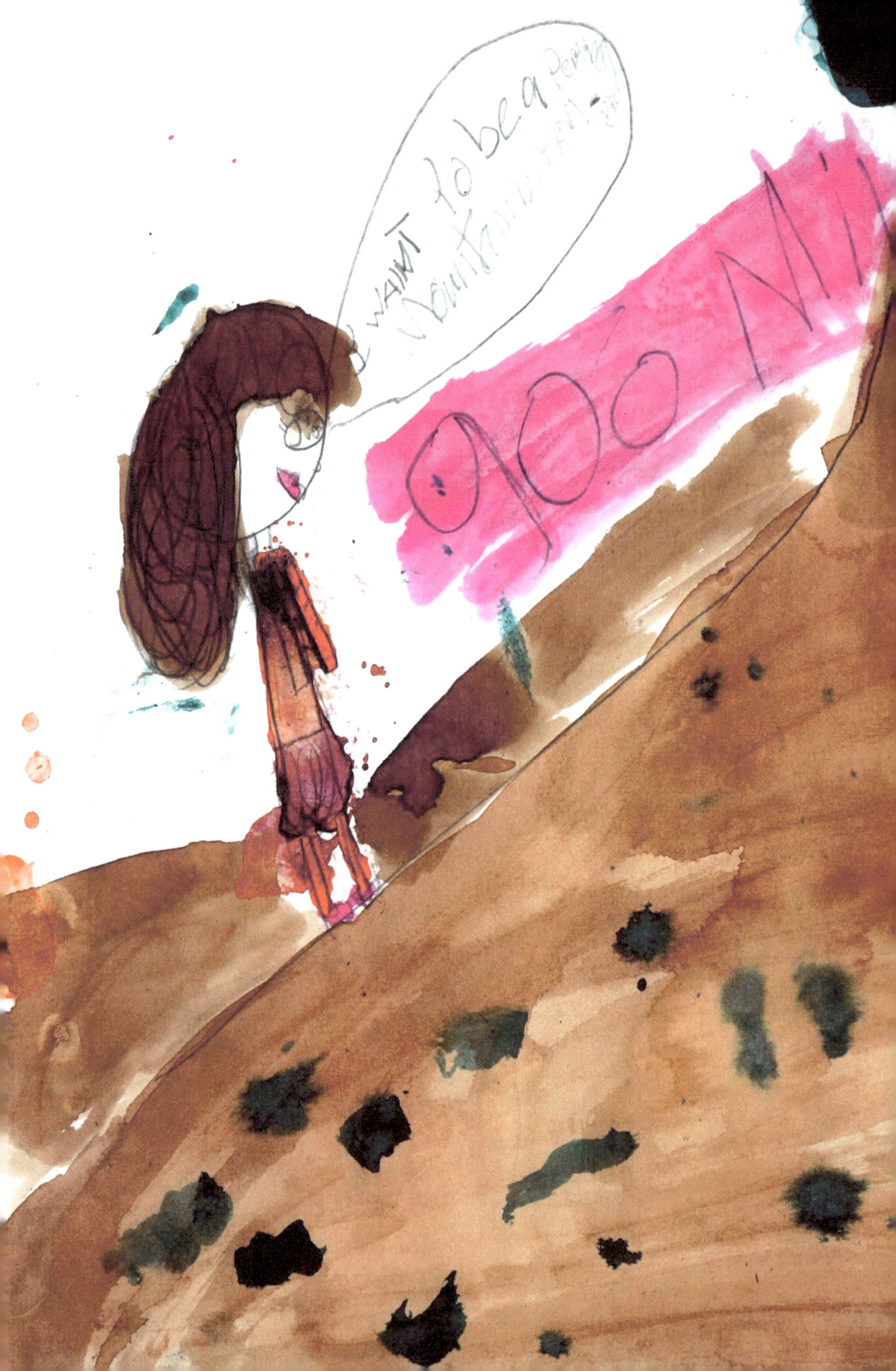

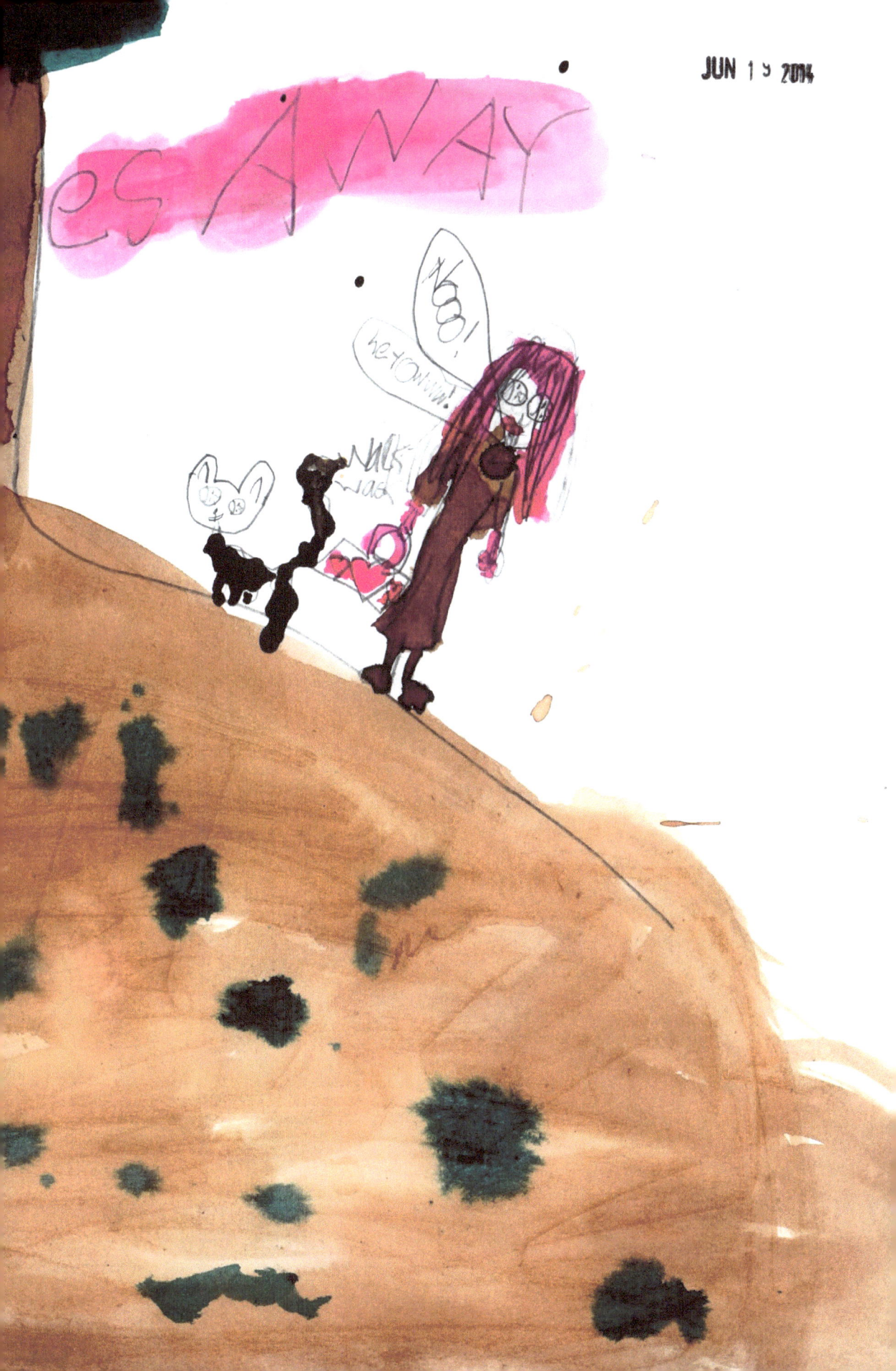

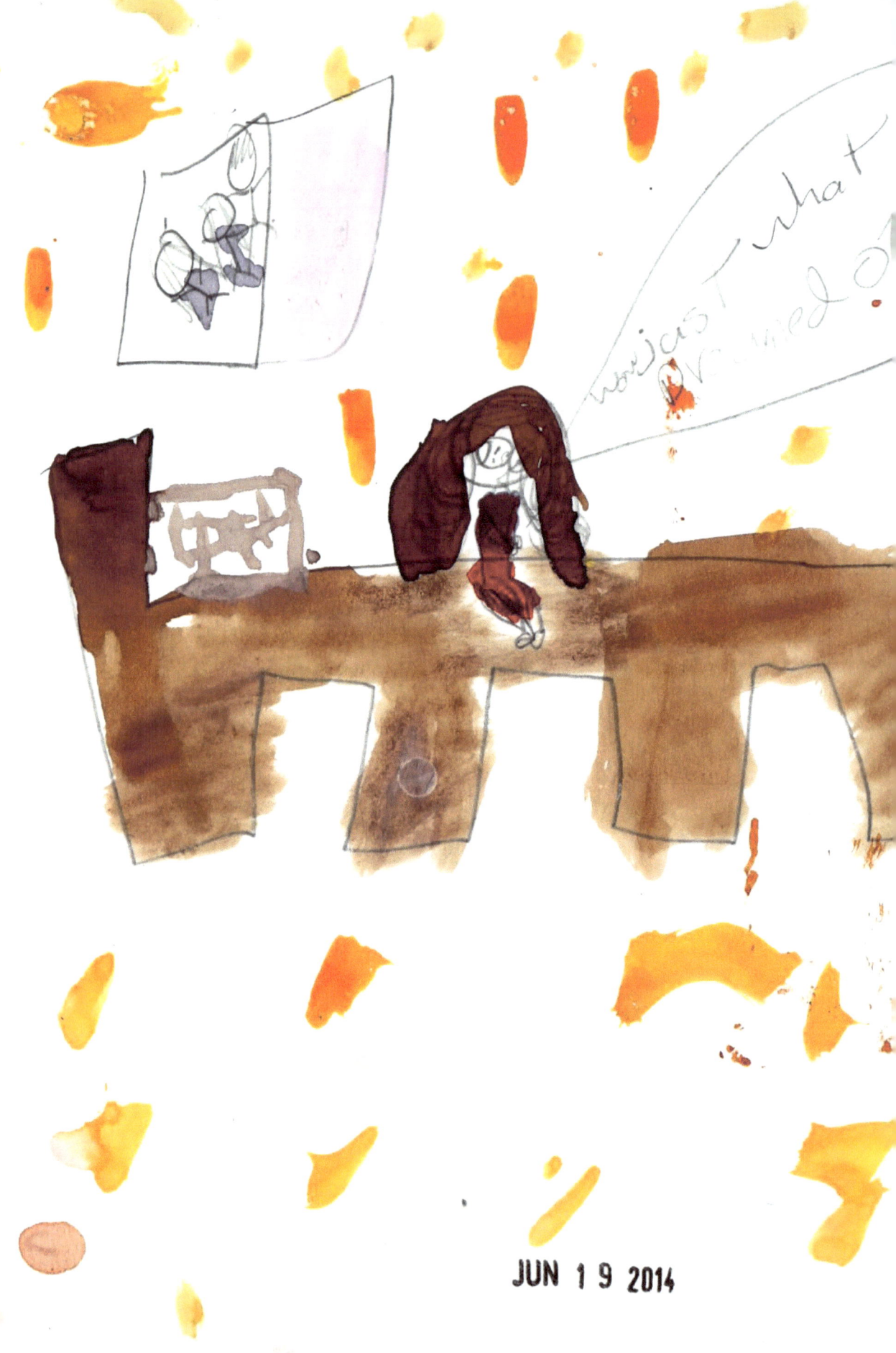

JUN 1 9 2014

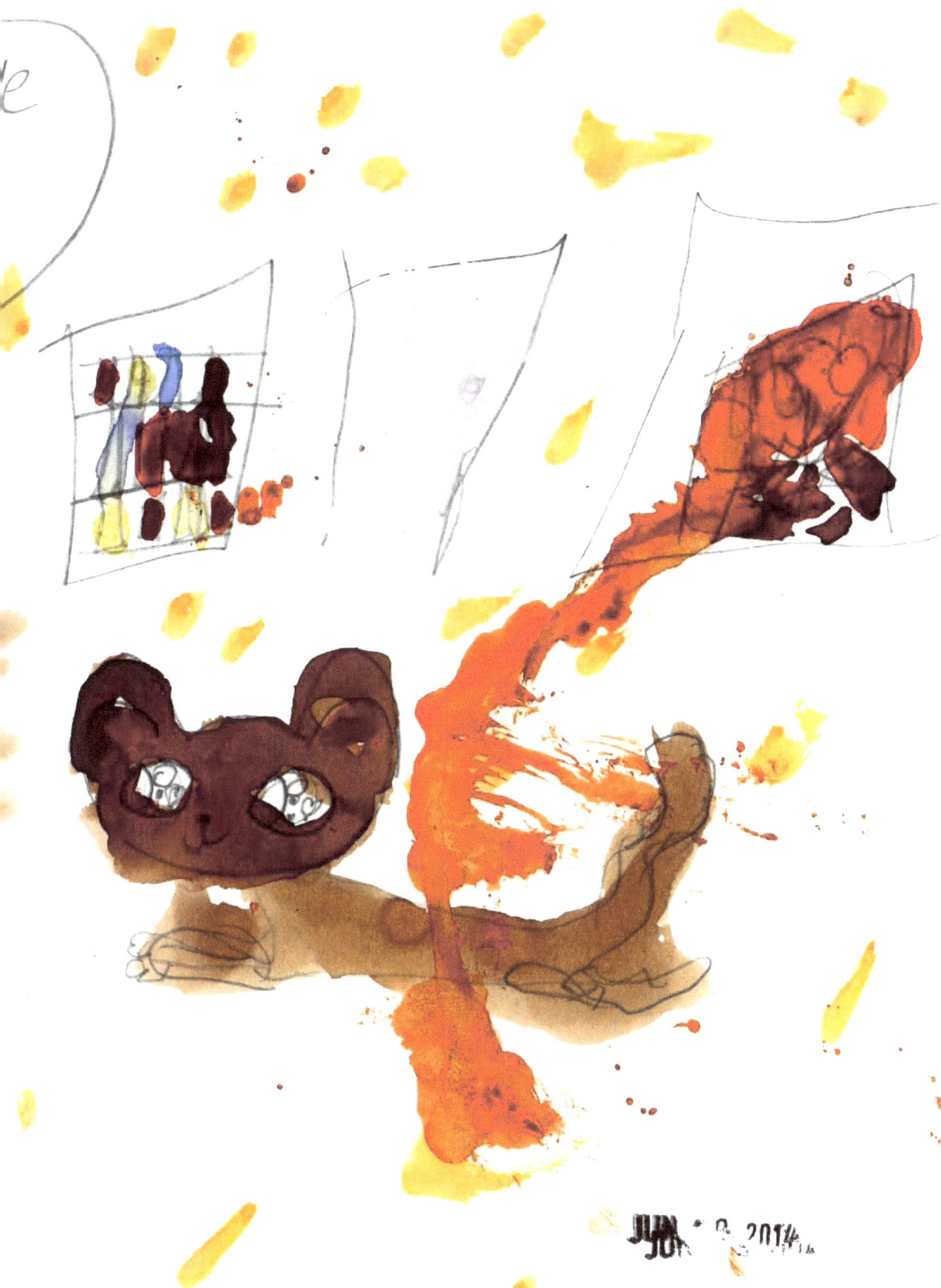

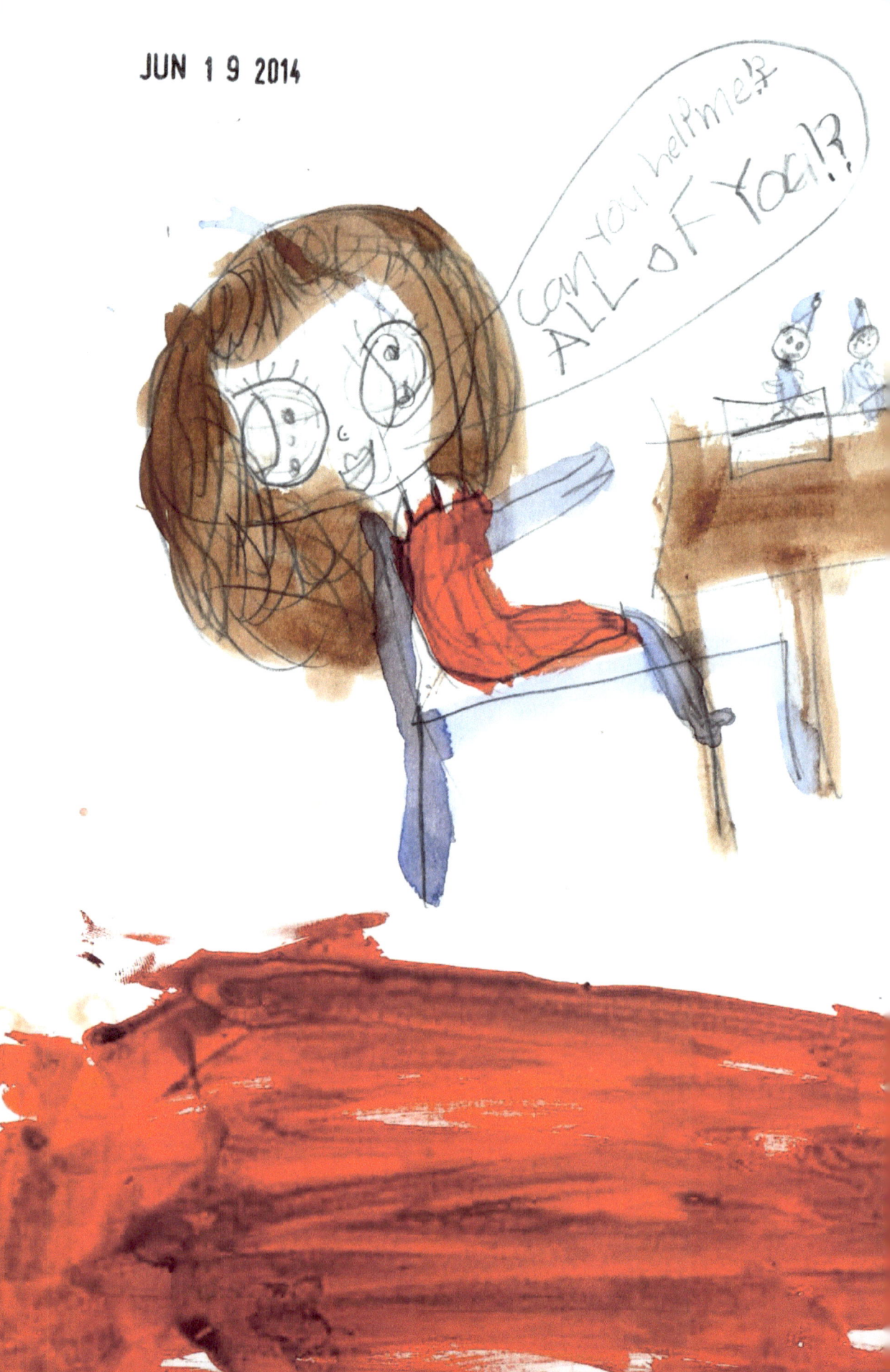

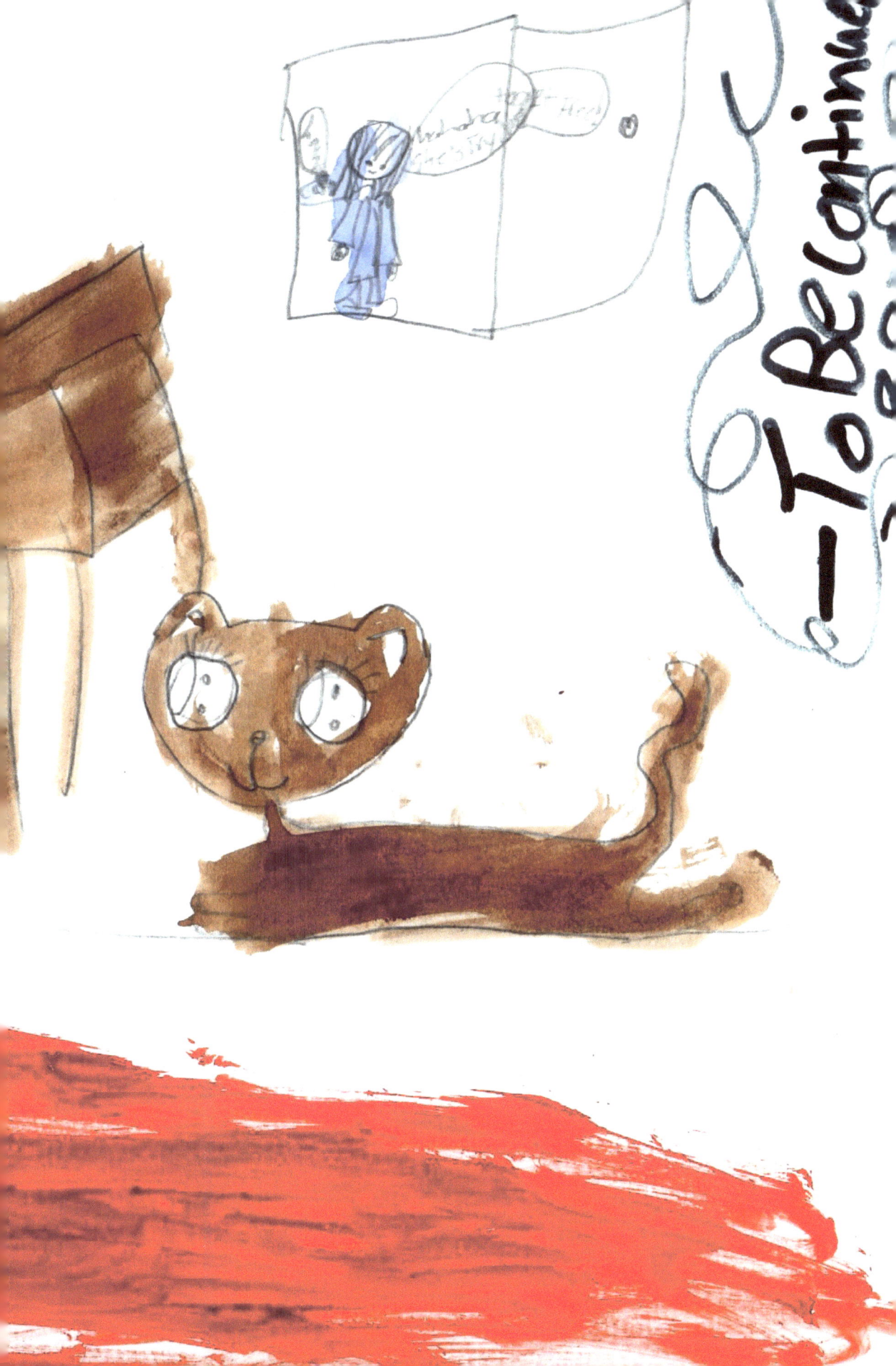

To Be continued

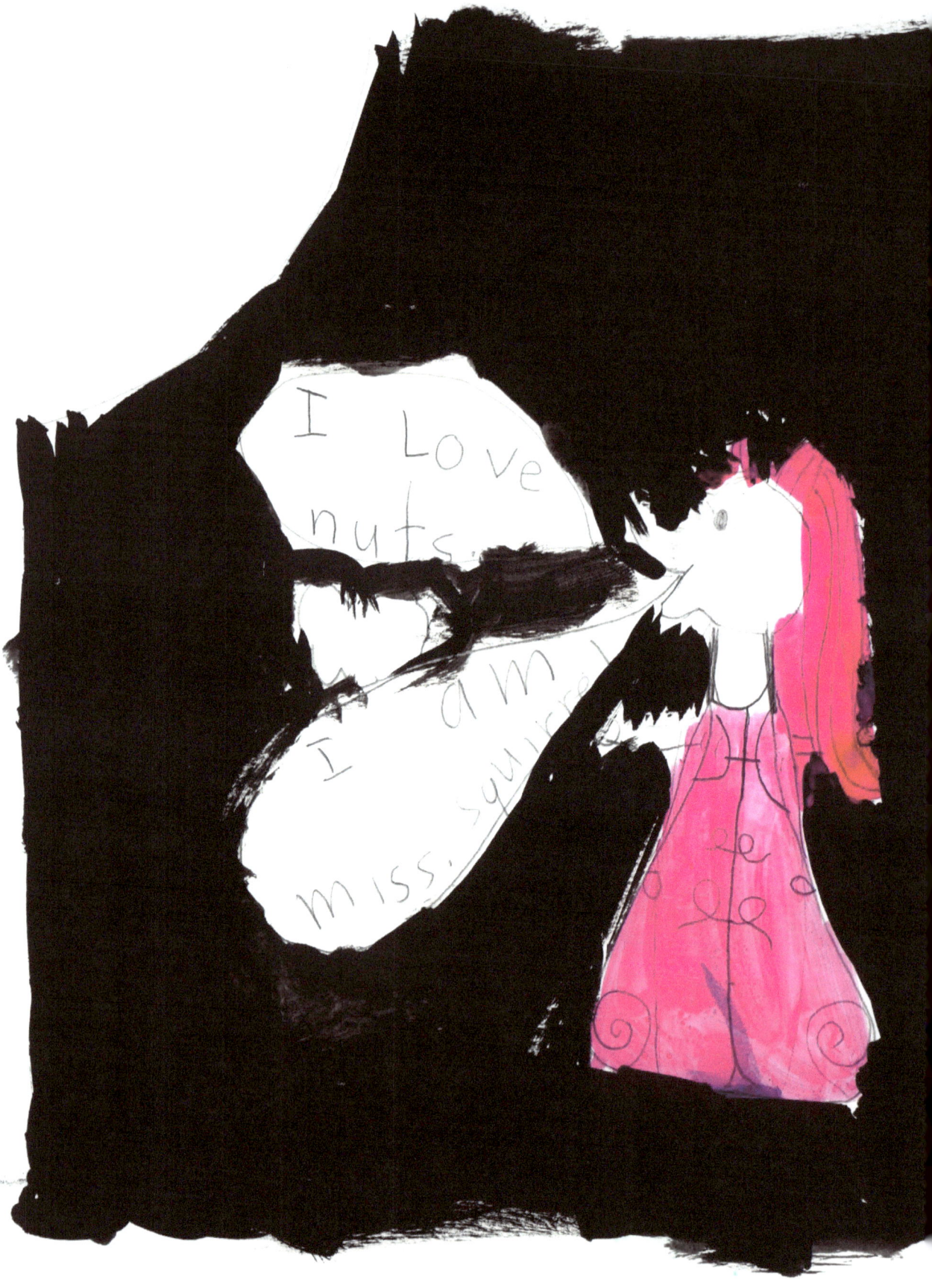

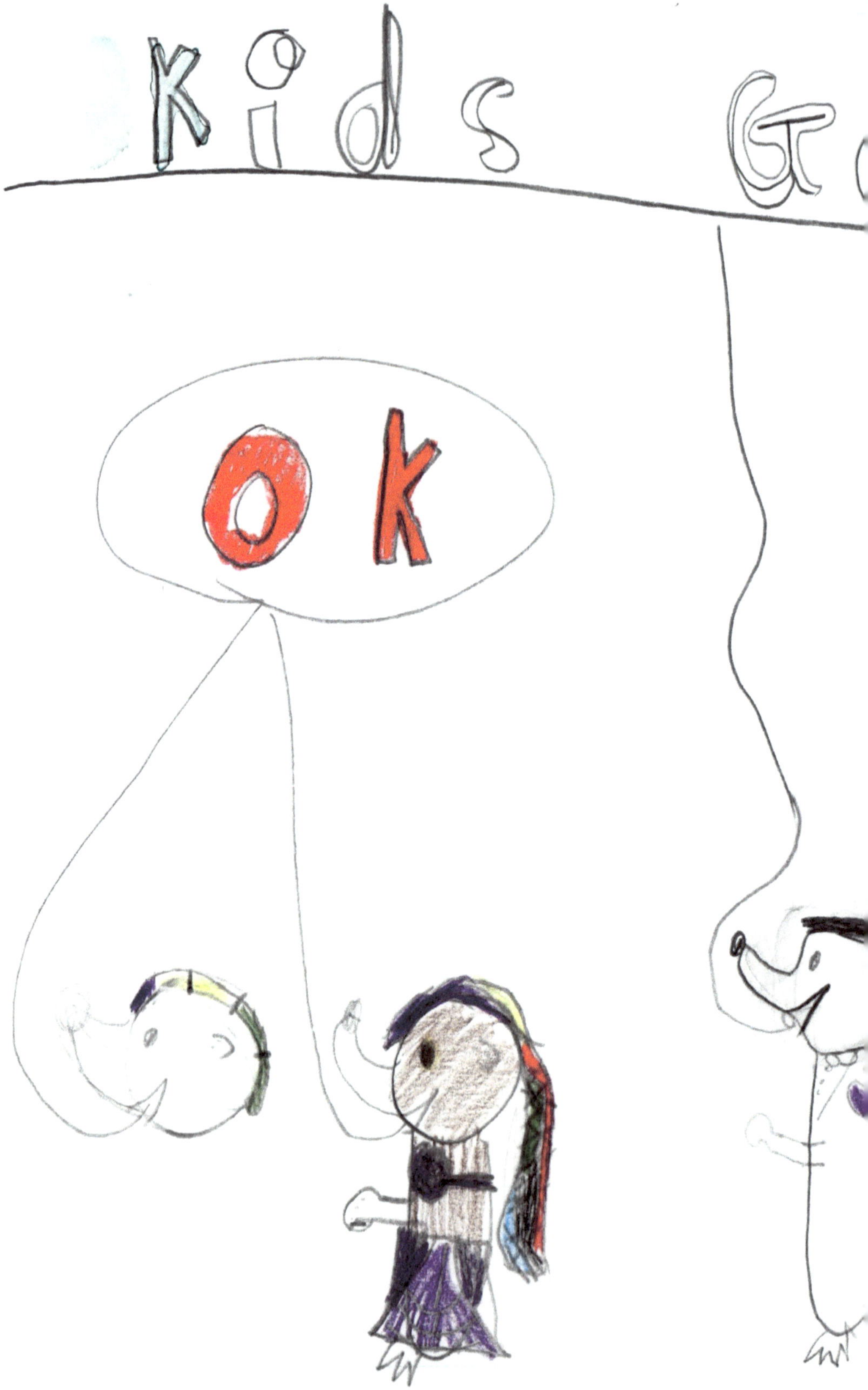
Kids
OK

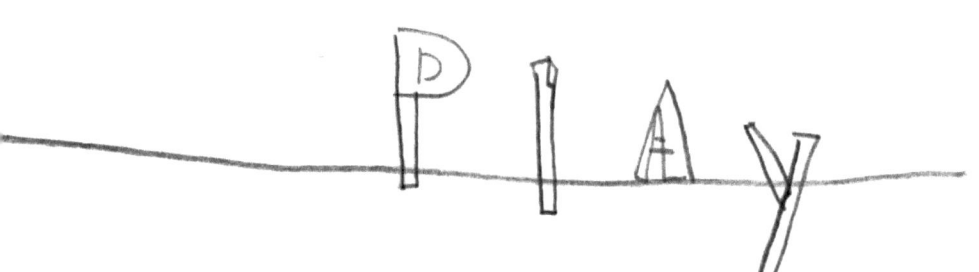

PlAy

G GG